A CONTRIBUTION TO THE GENERAL THEORY
OF COMPARATIVE LINGUISTICS

JANUA LINGUARUM

STUDIA MEMORIAE
NICOLAI VAN WIJK DEDICATA

edenda curat

C. H. VAN SCHOONEVELD

INDIANA UNIVERSITY

SERIES MINOR

83

1970

MOUTON

THE HAGUE · PARIS

A CONTRIBUTION TO
THE GENERAL THEORY OF
COMPARATIVE LINGUISTICS

by

RADOSLAV KATIČIĆ

UNIVERSITY OF ZAGREB

1970
MOUTON
THE HAGUE · PARIS

LIBRARY OF CONGRESS CATALOG CARD NUMBER: 77-110956

Printed in The Netherlands by Mouton & Co., Printers, The Hague.

PREFACE

It is the aim of this study to enter in a coherent form some reflections on the methodological foundations of comparative linguistics as we have inherited them from our esteemed predecessors. There are therefore no new facts presented in the following pages but only some insights into the mutual relations of well-known concepts and the true nature of familiar procedures. A better understanding of what we already know rather than the acquisition of new knowledge is what I hope this book will give the reader.

A full discussion of the opinions of traditional and modern linguists has not been attempted since it would have considerably increased the bulk of the book and made its systematic exposition more difficult to follow. A bibliography of works on comparative linguistics is intended to compensate to a certain extent this deficiency. Quotations in the text refer only to such literature as is most directly connected with the topics under discussion. The reader who wants information on recent works in this field will have to resort to the bibliography. This work is meant to be a contribution to the current discussion of historical linguistics, not a survey of it.

The following pages deal with a series of fundamental concepts and with the problems they involve. Examples are given only to the extent to which they were deemed necessary to illustrate the reasoning and they should be viewed only in that capacity.

I would like here to express my warm and cordial thanks to all those who in whatever way have helped me to write this monograph. Among them should be mentioned specially: Mr. Peter de

Ridder of the Mouton Publishing Company who gave me the idea to write it and encouraged my work whenever we met; Dr. Leonardo Spalatin, my friend and colleague at the Faculty of Philosophy of the Zagreb University who discussed with me some chapters in detail and gave me the courage to defy the language barrier; all friends and colleagues of the Linguistic Circle of Zagreb who discussed with me the principal topics of this monograph and helped much with their questions and remarks. And, last but not least, my students to whom I thank a lot for the stimulating atmosphere in my classes. It was my teaching in the first place which helped the ideas exposed in this book to mature. Thank be them all for whatever is good in the following pages. For the deficiencies the author alone is responsible.

Zagreb, October 1967   Radoslav Katičić

TABLE OF CONTENTS

1

INTRODUCTORY NOTES

The subject of comparative linguistics, or comparative philology, as it is called more traditionally, can be broadly defined as the study of genetic relationships between languages. It is true that the genetic approach is not the only one supplying a basis for the comparison of languages. But it is also a historical fact that until now they have mostly been compared on that basis and with remarkable success. Therefore the term 'comparative linguistics' even without any further qualification denotes in this study genetic work in linguistics.[1]

The comparative method as the main tool of comparative linguistics serves to find out the data that are thought relevant for the establishment of genetic relationships. The results obtained by such research permit the classification of the languages of the world in accordance with genetic criteria.

It is the purpose of this book to investigate the foundations of comparative linguistics in the light of recent views in linguistic theory. If this traditional field of linguistic studies is to become incorporated in a modern body of linguistic doctrine, the comparative method must be made explicit and its procedures must become more formal. If a method is stated explicitly it becomes possible to discern its properties and to show why it is successful and where it could be expected to fail. The results of such an inquiry may permit to rid the method of its weaknesses or to compensate for them. In this way it can be made still more successful

---

[1] Concerning the possibilities of comparing languages and the place that genetic-comparative linguistics occupies, cf. Ellis (1966).

and its results will become more universally applicable. The excellent results yielded by the comparative method in establishing the genetic relationships of some languages and its failure to provide sure criteria in other cases call for such an investigation of its theoretical premises.

It will be also interesting to see if modern linguistic theory is able to shed some light on the true nature of comparative procedures and to explain the relations of the comparative method to descriptive linguistics. Comparativists are traditionally inclined to believe that no language can be fully 'understood' without comparing it to other related languages and without knowing its history. This is most fervently denied by many descriptivists who maintain the view that comparison and history are irrelevant to description and hence to the 'understanding' of languages. Their contention seems logically impeccable. But is the intuitive consensus of traditional linguistics to be discarded altogether? This again can be answered only after the proposed investigation is completed and the comparative method is made more explicit.

It is a well-known fact that the marked interest in the genetic classification of languages prevailing in the last century and at the beginning of the present one had its root in European nationalism. The exact knowledge of genetic relationships of dialects and languages was supposed to strengthen the national individuality and to align nations in 'natural' alliances. To day, nations are more firmly established and so it has become easier to understand that genetic relationships of languages do not imply closeness of political outlook. Does this mean that comparative linguistics lose importance if they cannot be used profitably to such ends? It is quite possible, on the other hand, that comparative linguistics has some purely linguistic values. In other words, it may be universally applicable and not only to the ends that provided the emotional incentive for its inauguration. Any comparativist will be ready to confirm this. But his intuition can be proved right or wrong only if the implications, the premises and properties of the comparative method are correctly understood. For all these reasons, the proposed investigations seem very promising. They can contribute to the solution of many crucial problems of the linguistic science.

2

LINGUISTIC VARIETY AND THE RELATIONSHIP OF LANGUAGES

When we say that comparative linguistics tries to find out whether there is a genetic relationship between languages, we imply that other linguistic relationships exist which are not genetic. Therefore the discussion of the general notion of linguistic relationship is a necessary preliminary for any investigation of the comparative method.

The linguistic relationship implies a variety of languages, because the relationship of a language to itself, though very close, is trivial. It is the relationship of different languages that is worth investigating.

Any inquiry into the nature of linguistic variety presupposes, again, the concept of language itself. Many definitions of this concept have been proposed so far, but this does not relieve us from the obligation to give our own for the purposes of this investigation. From this point of view it seems most convenient to define language as an organization of texts. By text we understand the physical substance used in speech in order to convey the linguistic message from the performer (speaker) to the addressee (hearer), be it sound, light, electric impulses or any other physical substance. If this concept of language is accepted any particular language can be defined by the statement of its abstract organizational properties as presented in a workable model.[1]

In all essentials this definition of language is in agreement with the well-known Saussurian views based on the distinction between

---

[1] Cf. Chao (1962), Hartmann (1965), and Katičić (1966).

langue and *parole*. It is also in full accordance with information theory. Language, thus concieved, can be said to represent a special case of a code in which messages are given. But speech in our system of linguistic concepts does not correspond to message in information theory. A message is a particular choice among the possibilities provided by the code. It is therefore no more material than the code itself. The concept of message in information theory has as its linguistic counterpart the particular choices among the possibilities provided by language. Such a choice is in its turn no more material than language itself is. The particular choices we shall call LINGUISTIC UNITS. This broad and general term denotes already in its accepted meaning all possible choices a language provides on different levels.

A linguistic unit, which may in itself be a string of smaller linguistic units, corresponds to the concept of message in information theory. In fact, a linguistic unit is a special, a linguistic case of a message.

A CHANNEL is according to the terminology of information theory the physical substance that every message needs in order to be dispatched from the source to the receiver. In our system of linguistic concepts speech and its texts correspond to the channel of information theory.

Between linguistic units and texts or segments of texts there is a definite relation. This relation we shall call REALIZATION and we shall say that linguistic units are realized in texts or in segments of texts.[2]

There is a certain reluctance among a part of linguists to accept the distinction between linguistic unit and text, but it is easy to show that the distinction is necessary. Nobody will deny that the same linguistic unit may occur in different texts. And as nothing can be simultaneously identical and non-identical, the linguistic unit must be distinguished from the physical substance of the text in which it is realized. In that case one can say that the same linguistic unit is realized in different texts or segments of texts. This

[2]   Cf. Šaumjan (1962, 36ff.).

is fully in accordance with our intuitive ideas about language and it makes it possible for us to explain the empirical fact that in different instances of speach the same can be said.

In recent times it has become increasingly common to define a language as a set of sentences.[3] But since this set is infinite, no particular language can be defined by enumerating its sentences. It is therefore necessary to state what conditions sentences must fulfill in order to be recognized as belonging to a certain set. In other words, their organization must be described. This shows clearly that both definitions of language: as a set of sentences and as the organization of texts are in fact equivalent.[4]

It is necessary now to analyze in some detail the implications our definition of language has for the concepts of LINGUISTIC VARIETY and of LINGUISTIC RELATIONSHIP. The concept of linguistic variety is needed in order to account for the empirical fact that a person able to produce and to understand some texts can practically never do so with every existing text. This means that all texts are not organized in the same way or, in other words, that there is more than one language. This again is in full accordance with our intuitive ideas.

Linguistic variety is a set of all languages that can be perceived as different. This means that dialects and even idiolects will appear as members of this set. This is only consistent with our definition of language which implies the annulment of a distinction among dialect, idiolect and language. Dialects and idiolects, being recognizably different organizations of texts, must be accepted as different languages in the linguistic variety set. In fact, it is necessary, at least in theory, to disregard for our purposes, this traditional distinction if any strictness is to be attained in the system of our concepts. For there is no clearcut general criterion by which dialect can be distinguished from language.

The traditional classification is based on a subjective and arbitrary evaluation of how much different organizations of texts

[3] Cf. Chomsky (1957, 13).
[4] Cf. Chomsky (1964, 10) about the Saussurian implications of his linguistic theory.

are and of their respective social, political and cultural importance. Therefore it is impossible to prove that two given organizations of texts should be considered as dialects of one language if this happens to be contested. In many cases it is much easier to show that the differences between two given organizations of texts are evidently so far-reaching that it is impossible to consider them as dialects of one language. Until this whole complex is thoroughly investigated and the necessary criteria found, the only solution for linguistic theory is to disregard the distinction.

It is of course practically impossible to work with a variety set containing all languages that can be perceived as different. This means that many observable differences will have to be disregarded in practice. This is the only way in which all practical investigations become possible. The investigator is free to state the criteria of identity as they best suit his purpose. But these criteria must be explicit and as general as possible. In our case it would be preferable if it were possible to establish a general unit of language difference. Then it could be stated in a general way and without individual specifications which differences will be disregarded for every investigation.

Unfortunately, the setting of such a unit presupposes again a general objective criterion for the estimation of differences among languages. As our present knowledge does not make it possible for us to set up such criteria,[5] we shall be constrained to introduce in the linguistic variety set the whole subjective traditional language classification with its arbitrary distinctions between languages and dialects. But we shall do so explicitly while stressing that no general criterion underlies the inherited classification and that the differences that are regarded as relevant are to be listed individually because no general statement about them is possible. In doing so, we shall always remember how unsatisfactory this classification is from a stricter theoretical point of view. But no very serious harm should be feared from our using it in our pre-

---

[5]   For some ideas in this direction cf. Greenberg (1955, 1956, 1957a, 1957, 1960), Kroeber (1960a and 1960b), Voegelin-Ramanujan-Voegelin (1960), Housholder (1960), Lieberson (1964).

liminary considerations since it embodies an intuitive approach to language analysis profitably applied through centuries and it would be unwise to underestimate its value.

In working with the linguistic variety set we have thus a great freedom. Any language that can be perceived as different from all others may be a member of the set if we choose so. But we are also at liberty to disregard any difference if we think it convenient. So we shall be free to investigate all properties of the language variety set and we can hope to find at some future time a strict and adequate method for setting identity criteria for its members.

The concept of a linguistic variety set as sketched above implies that a language is a discrete unit and the languages of two sets of texts can be either identical or different and nothing else. According to this theory, there can be no continuum of sameness and non-sameness in the organization of texts. Wherever any difference can be detected the languages are to be ruled different except for the differences which are to be disregarded by explicit identity criteria. This is a necessary consequence of the assumption, prevailing in the linguistic theory of our days, that the facts of speech are best accounted for by discrete constructs. If language is a set of discrete constructs, it must itself be a construct and discrete.

Once it is accepted that the linguistic unit has to be distinguished from the text in which it is realized, it becomes impossible to state any positive definition of linguistic units as long as we stick to the taxonomic theory of descriptive linguistics.[6] According to it language is most adequately modelled as an inventory of units and a set of rules containing the restrictions in their distribution in strings which in their turn form units of a higher rank. If the units cannot be defined by the properties of the substance in which they are realized, every unit is defined only by its obligatory non-sameness with all the other units in the inventory to which it belongs.[7] This means that every unit in an inventory is defined by

[6] For the term, cf. Chomsky (1964, 11).
[7] There was an attempt in descriptive linguistics to reduce the relation of obligatory non-sameness to differences in distribution, but it was not fully successful. Cf. *e.g.* Harris (1951, § 7.3).

all other units. Hence it follows that no same units can be found in different languages. If every item is defined by its non-sameness with the other items in the inventory there can be no same units in different inventories. This can be shown on a simple example. Suppose two inventories = A {a, b} and = B {a, c}. In this case a, member of A, is different from a, member of B, because the first is defined by $\neq$ a b and the second by $\neq$ a c. The item a in the two inventories is not identical in spite of its identical expression in our symbolic language and whatever closeness in other respects this may mean. Consequently the languages in the variety set are absolutely different and have no common units.

By this implication the taxonomic linguistic theory fails to account for the intuitively well-known empirical fact that all languages are not different to the same degree. So, for instance, High German differs notably from Low German both in the inventory and in the distribution of phonemes and morphemes. According to the taxonomic theory they ought to be two totally different languages. And yet it is evident that they are much less different one from the other than they both are from, say, Hungarian. The same can be said of Slovenian and Serbo-Croatian. They, too, differ in the inventory and in the distribution of phonemes and morphemes and are consequently totally different in terms of the taxonomic language theory. And again this difference is in reality much lesser than the difference between any one of them and Basque.

Whereas the diversity among the languages in the variety set is unrestricted in terms of the taxonomic linguistic theory, the empirical fact of mutual understandability of languages that are distinctly different and the process of language learning induce us to assume the existence of restrictions on linguistic diversity. In other words, every adequate linguistic theory has to account for the fact that different languages are not always as different as they could be. In order to meet this requirement, the taxonomic linguistic theory has to make use of the concept of CORRESPONDENCE.

Units of different languages may correspond, and it is this correspondence that restricts linguistic diversity. The correspondence relation can be even included into the criteria for language identity, and in that case correspondent units are accepted as identical. A unit can thus belong to more than one language. The diversity of languages having common units and distributions is accordingly restricted. In principle it is possible to measure the extent of these restrictions by counting the common units of two or more languages. But this unity of measure is of little practical value because it is very difficult to survey and to count the correspondent units on all levels. In spite of this difficulty, the classification of different organizations of texts in languages, dialects and idiolects is in traditional linguistics theoretically accounted for just by such unexhaustive counting of correspondences.

It is important to point out that because of these restrictions in linguistic diversity and its resulting graduality the languages concerned do not cease to be discrete units. Their variety set does not become a continuum since linguistic diversity is restricted by the correspondence of units which are themselves discrete.

In generative transformational linguistic theory, as often advocated recently,[8] the whole setting of the problem is different. In this approach language is not modelled as a set of classes of units with specified restrictions on their distribution but as a partly ordered set of rules generating linguistic units which are in their turn strings of smaller units. Such models, too, are organized in levels but in levels of rules and not in levels of units.

In generating the infinite set of grammatical sentences of a given language the transformational generative models start from a universal unit symbolized by S.[9] All languages begin the generation of their grammatical sentences with this symbol, hence it represents every grammatical sentence of all languages in the variety set. These languages differ only in the rules[10] by which actual sentences are generated. It follows that the sets of rules

[8] Cf. Chomsky (1964, 9 and 11 ff., 1965, 63 ff.).
[9] Cf. Chomsky (1957, 29 and 1961, 121).
[10] Cf. Chomsky (1961).

modelling the different languages in the variety set have at least one element in common: the initial symbol S.

Two languages are identical to the extent to which their models provide identical operations by which they generate their strings from S or from any other point which can be defined universally in the process of generation. The generative rules are the units of such a model and their identity depends not only on the sameness of the generative operation for which they contain instructions but also on the sameness of the generative history of the strings to which these operations apply. Whereas the units of taxonomic language models are only negatively defined by their obligatory non-sameness with all other units in the inventory, the rules of a transformational generative grammar can be defined positively by their position in reference to S or to any other universally defined point in the process of generation and by the identity of the intervening rules on the partly ordered set. From this difference between the models follows another one very important from our point of view. While it is logically impossible for taxonomic models of different languages to have units in common, it is possible for transformational generative models to have a common subset of rules. Every rule that appears in more than one grammar restricts the diversity of languages.

In order to account for the empirically-given restrictions on linguistic diversity the transformational generative linguistic theory is not obliged to resort to the additional concept of correspondence. Grammars with a common subset of rules necessarily generate sentences which show correspondence relations. The concept of correspondence is thus implicit in the notion of common rules shared by two or more transformational generative models. Moreover, the number of rules appearing as common elements in the models of two languages provides a means to measure objectively the extent to which linguistic variety is restricted. It is much easier to survey and count the identical rules in two generative grammars than to do the same with corresponding units in two taxonomic descriptions. On these lines a criterion for the distinction of dialects from genetically related languages could eventually be found.

The ease linguistic variety is dealt with in terms of transformational generative models and the obvious unit of measurement for the restrictions imposed on linguistic diversity it offers provide strong additional arguments for the greater explanatory power of the transformational generative linguistic theory.

There is one basic difficulty in applying the unit of measurement for linguistic diversity discussed above: alternative transformational generative models for a language are possible and they may differ substantially as to the subset of rules they have in common with the model of another language. Moreover, this set can always be enlarged at the expense of the simplicity of the model. This serious difficulty can be overcome only by an additional requirement to the effect that the models in which the common rules are counted should be the most adequate of those brought forward for both languages whose relationship is to be measured. Such a requirement is possible since the evaluation of alternative models as a task of linguistic theory is undisputable.[11]

In its present state linguistic theory is unable to offer even a criterion by which one can decide whether a proposed model is the best for the language of a given corpus. We can only choose the most adequate from a number of alternative models. This means that we can never tell if a more adequate new model may not appear. It is therefore necessary to have always an open mind for a re-evaluation of language relationship as established by counting the common generative rules in models that at a certain moment were judged to be the most adequate of all so far proposed for a set of languages. Linguistic relationships are the subject of continuous investigation whose results must be reconsidered in the light of every new idea that may prove significant for the theory of descriptive models.

The genetic relationships of languages, as established and investigated by comparative linguistics, are a special case of restricted linguistic diversity. Not every linguistic relationship can be qualified as genetic and there are many cases of related lan-

[11] Cf. Chomsky (1957, 50ff.).

guages whose relationship is not genetic. There are two generally recognized types of non-genetic linguistic relationships. One of them is usually labelled typological. For the other there is no generally accepted label. As it is allegedly the result of the so-called linguistic loan, whatever this may mean, we shall call it loan relationship.

It is easy to distinguish neatly genetic and loan relationship since the first is a relationship by origin and the second by contact. Although both concepts at closer examination raise a host of difficult problems, they form, at least in principle, a clear-cut opposition, the one being primary and the other secondary. Less clear is the distinction between either of them and typological relationship. Even before the notions of the three types of linguistic relationship are subjected to closer scrutiny it is obvious that in this tripartition there is no consistent *principium divisionis*. While genetic and loan relationships are defined by the way they came about, typological relationship is determined by the way it manifests itself. This immediately raises two questions. The first is: how do genetic and loan relationships manifest themselves? And the second: how does typological relationship come about? It is not difficult to conceive a typological relationship resulting from common origin or from contact. In such a case one and the same restriction of linguistic variety could simultaneously be typological and genetic or a loan relationship.

It is quite usual in linguistics to regard languages as related in more than one way. English and French *e.g.*, are genetically related and also by loan and typologically. This is true only for the languages as a whole but not for the individual restrictions on their diversity, *i.e.*, for their individual correspondences. The correspondence between *mother* and *mère* is classified as genetic relationship and nothing else while *voice* and *voix* is described only as loan relationship. The fact, that in both languages the difference between the use of a substantive as subject or as object in a sentence is marked by the order of words only and by no change in their phonemic shape, is an example of purely typological relationship. In the case of the individual correspondence *voice* and *voix* it is impossible to ask whether this correspondence while being due to loan relationship (contact) could simultaneously be a consequence of genetic relationship (common origin). Such a question is logically inadmissible because common origin and contact, as conceived in linguistics, exclude each other. But it is by no means contrary to logic to ask whether the typological correspondence in the marking of the difference between subject and object may perhaps be an instance of genetic or loan relationship.

On the other hand, Hungarian and Turkish correspond in the way they express grammatical categories. By this correspondence a typological relationship of these languages is established. But the question whether it may be due to common origin and hence be an instance of genetic relationship is very heatedly disputed until the present day. It follows that genetic and loan relationship on one side and typological relationship on the other do not logically exclude each other.

In order to gain a clearer insight into the true nature of the different kinds of linguistic relationships it is necessary to subject them to closer scrutiny and to make the underlaying principles of division explicit and consistent. Typology is a classification according to some shared features that are for some reason considered characteristic and important and are therefore selected as relevant for the classification. In this sense every linguistic relationship is typological because linguistic relationship is nothing else but corresponding features shared by two or more members of the linguistic variety set.

The conclusion that every linguistic relationship is typological is in full accordance with the view commonly held on typological relationship. It is readily explained as common or correspondent features in the organization of languages. But having defined language as the organization of texts, all correspondent features of languages must by logical necessity be features of organization. Genetic and loan relationships must hence be regarded as two special cases of typological relationship. But it is common linguistic knowledge that Serbo-Croatian and Bulgarian are more closely related genetically than either of them is with Russian, whereas Russian and Serbo-Croatian have a higher degree of typological relationship than either of them has with Bulgarian. It follows clearly from this proposition that there a typological relationship is meant that does not include genetic relationship. In accepting the legacy of European linguistic tradition we must distinguish two different meanings of 'typological relationship'. One, broader, includes genetic and loan relationship and the other, narrower, excludes both.[12] In full accordance with tradition, the term can be reserved for the narrower meaning because the broader meaning is synonymous with plain linguistic relationship which is necessarily typological in the general sense of the term.

It remains to define the narrower sense of typological relationship as used in linguistics. The mention of it immediately evokes the familiar classification of languages into synthetic and analytic, into inflexional, agglutinative, incorporating and isolating types. In the beginnings of comparative linguistics this typological classification was not clearly distinguished from the establishment of genetic relationship.[13] The typology underlaying this division is in fact a typology of the rules by which lexical and grammatical morphemes are combined into words. But in spite of the outstanding importance of such morphological typology, it cannot be accepted as the sole criterion of typology in the narrower sense. There have been also typological studies in phonology and in syntax. All these comparative studies try to establish correspondences of system equivalence.[14] The more equivalent traits can be shown to exist in the languages compared, the closer is their typological relationship.

Genetic and typological relationships differ in the kind of correspondences by which they are established. In comparative linguistics such correspondences are established for which it may be assumed that they are a consequence of a common origin. The correspondent terms may or may not be equivalent in the respective systems of the languages compared. In typology, only equiv-

---

[12] Cf. Uspenskij (1965, 23 and 30).
[13] Cf. Schlegel (1808).
[14] Cf. Bazell (1958), Milewski (1963, 5) and Skalička (1963, 32ff.).

alent terms are acknowledged as correspondent and they may or may not be of common origin.

The above discussion shows that it is possible to distinguish neatly between linguistic typology in its narrower sense and comparative linguistics by virtue of a clear-cut difference in the correspondence relations they accept as relevant. But it is impossible to find such a criterion in order to distinguish them both from loan relationship. The correspondences resulting from the contact of languages are by themselves and without additional information indistinguishable from mere typological or genetic correspondences. There is no difference between the kind of correspondence in *mother* : *mère* and in *voice* : *voix*. Only additional information linguistic and extralinguistic, allow us to decide that the former is to be classified as genetic and the second as a loan relationship. One of the main subjects of this book is to find out what this additional information, required for such a decision, consists of (cf. chapter 6).

Languages in contact show a marked tendency to increase the number of equivalent units in the system. The comparative with *more* and *most* in English, the rich case system in Ossetic, the lack of grammatical gender in Armenian and of an infinitive in Bulgarian are examples of loan relationships manifesting themselves as typological relationships. Without additional information it is by no means possible to distinguish such cases from other typological correspondences occurring among the most remote languages of the world with no contacts whatsoever as, *e.g.*, Chinese and Ewe in West Africa both having tones. From this it follows that a typological correspondence may be at the same time a loan correspondence by the way it came about whereas a genetic correspondence cannot simultaneously be a loan correspondence.

This tripartition of linguistic relationship provides a variety of seven different ways in which languages may be related:

	I	II	III	IV	V	VI	VII	VIII
typological	+	+	+	+	—	—	—	—
genetic	+	+	—	—	+	+	—	—
by loan	+	—	+	—	+	—	+	—

All possibilities provided by our theory of linguistic relationship occur actually in the variety set of languages if typological relationship is taken in the narrower sense. In order to prove this it will suffice to quote an instance for every possibility: I English and French, II Latin and Sanskrit, III Arabic and Serbo-Croatian, IV Chinese and Ewe, V English and Hindi, VI Ancient Greek and Modern Persian, VII Chinese and Japanese, VIII Chinese and Swahili. In this sketch the non-existence of genetic relationship means only that such a relationship has as yet not been established for it is impossible to demonstrate that two languages are not related genetically.

Because of the existence of very important linguistic universals there are no typologically altogether unrelated languages.[15] Therefore, in typological classification, such languages are regarded as unrelated which besides the universals have no important typological correspondences, *i.e.*, no such correspondences as have so far been chosen as classification criteria in typological research. It is in this sense that the lack of typological relationship in the adduced instances should be understood. It is an important task for linguistic typology to find exact criteria by which languages can be classified as typologically related or unrelated.

In a similar way the absence of loan relationship in our instances is not to be interpreted as absolute lack of loans. In such a case our example for II could be discarded because Latin and Sanskrit share the loanword *dēnārius dīnāra* and others. Similar objections could be made in the case of other instances cited above. But few scattered accidental loanwords are not enough to classify two languages as related by loan. Here again it is impossible to give exact criteria, but as much can be said that loans, whether lexical or typological, must be numerous and important enough for them to be accepted as evidence of a direct and intense cultural contact. Although this formulation is not too satisfactory from a theoretical point of view, it expresses exactly the current procedure as applied in language classification and it is in full accordance with the in-

[15] Cf. Greenberg (1963) and Chomsky (1965, 35 ff.).

tuitive knowledge we have of linguistic phenomena. The difference between languages sharing some loan words and deep historical loan relationships is in practice mostly evident. It remains a small number of border cases in which it may be difficult to find a satisfactory criterion to distinguish them.

It would be easy to formalize the criteria by classifying as related any two languages having any typological correspondences beyond the universals or any loan correspondence, even if it is a minor typological feature or a single loan word. The result would be a theoretically neat situation. But typological and loan relationship would, so defined, be of little interest. The formal neatness would be paid for by a complete failure to make the distinctions which alone can help to a deeper understanding of language relationship. There is no doubt that further research will clarify many of these concepts. But even as things are now, it is for most practical purposes possible to handle satisfactorily the principal concepts underlying the classification of languages. Less important and scattered typological and loan correspondences must therefore be ignored in a general classification of languages.

It is the task of this book to set up an explicit theory of genetic relationships between languages, comprising the whole rich experience gathered in this field by the linguistic science. The fundamental concepts connected with genetic relationship are therefore to be thoroughly investigated and it must be shown to what extent they can be conceived as discrete units and where a statistic approximation is needed.

According to the theory sketched above, genetic relationship of languages is a special case of restricted linguistic diversity. Generally, it is defined as partial correspondence due to common origin. Therefore it will be necessary to investigate the notions of origin and descent in linguistics and to see how it can be clearly distinguished from borrowing which provides another kind of restrictions on linguistic diversity.

On the other hand, common origin of languages can never be established by direct observation. It can only be inferred from a special kind of characteristic correspondences. An inquiry into the fundamental notion of correspondence is essential for any statement of an explicit theory of genetic relationship in linguistics. It is necessary, also, to distinguish genetic correspondences from typological ones and to specify the conditions that must be fulfilled if a set of languages is to be regarded as genetically related.

As genetic relationships of languages occur in time and space, among socially organized speakers, they are to be considerated also in this connection. Twofold are the questions that arise in connection with this subject. It must be seen whether and how inferences can be drawn from established genetic relationships of languages for extralinguistic history and if and what extralinguistic data can be relevant for the establishment of genetic relationship between languages. This is a very wide field of study and in the frame of a small book it will be possible only to touch upon the fundamental problems. The final part of this book will be devoted to an explicit theory of the genetic classification of languages.

3

LANGUAGE CHANGE AND LINGUISTIC DESCENT

One of the basic facts about languages, as we see them now, is their constant change. Even during the life span of an individual, his speech habits undergo observable alterations. Texts that were easily understood in a community become unintelligible in the course of time. No community is able to produce spontanuously for a longer period texts with the same organization. The concept of language change is introduced in order to account for these empirical facts. But it is highly significant that language change has only very recently become a popular notion. For centuries, it was completely ignored by linguistic theory and common sense alike. For both, there were only different but unchanging languages in the world. Only the strong impact of the nineteenth century historical outlook made the idea of changing languages a familiar one to cultivated people.

If we examine the older notion of different but not changing languages from the point of view of our linguistic theory as sketched here, we shall be surprised to find it quite understandable and natural, whereas the concept of language change leads to complex theoretical difficulties.

When a community changes the organization of its texts, this can, in the terms of our linguistic theory, be regarded only as the substitution of one language for another.[1] Both languages are

---

[1] If we accept the basic theoretical premises of generative grammar, the substitution of languages must be viewed as a substitution of generative models, *i.e.*, grammars expressed by an ordered set of rules generating sentences. The substitution of G_j for G_i can be interpreted as the addition of a new subset of

members of the variety set and none of them has undergone any change in this operation. Of course, what resulted was a change, but it was a change in the relations between languages and communities rather than a change in the languages themselves. From this it follows that such changes are not linguistic but extralinguistic. There is no change in linguistic entities.

It could be maintained that such a change may be one in the linguistic variety set and that it should therefore be considered linguistically relevant. But even in the case when the new language had been nowhere used before a community substituted it for another, it is not necessary to assume that any change occurred in the variety set. For this set is independent of time in the sense that no simultanuous use in speech is postulated for its members. It includes all perceivably different languages without regard for the point in time when their texts were produced. This means that the linguistic variety set has as its members the organizations of all texts that are produced in the present, that were produced in the past or will be produced in the future. For any given portion of the time-space continuum a linguistic variety set can be stated, but it will be only a subset of the universal variety set. The substitution of one language for another in the use of a community affects only the extralinguistically determined subsets and not the variety set itself. So, even if the variety set is taken into consideration, language change must be regarded as an extralinguistic phenomenon.

As for the observable facts of language substitution in social communities, they can be fully accounted for by the notion of linguistic variety only. When a substitution of languages takes place in a community, what is actually observed are coexistent texts in different languages. The alteration of their respective frequency of appearance can only exceptionally be perceived because this requires the comparison of a great deal of data and attentive observation over a long period of time. In the light of

---

rules E_{i-j} to G_1, so that G_1 with the added rules E_{i-j} generates the same sentences as G_j. These additional rules are called extension rules. Cf. Halle (1962, 342-352); Klima (1964, 2); Isenberg (1965, 144-152).

these considerations the old view, according to which only different but unchanging languages exist, seems to be much less absurd than we are used to think.

The notion of changing languages becomes necessary only when we, for some purpose, disregard the difference among certain languages and look at them as one language with some internal variety. The concept of language change is not necessary to account for the substitution of Middle English for Old English in certain communities of the British Isles. But it becomes necessary when we want to maintain that Old and Middle English are in some way one and the same language. As they are evidently not, we say that they are one changing language, Old English being its earlier and Middle English its later stage. The notion of language change is not introduced in order to diversify languages but to impose restrictions on their variety. This is in fact the great achievement of the nineteenth century linguistics. It introduced the notion of language change in order to classify languages in accordance with some restrictions imposed on their variety.

It is easy to understand how important this discovery was at the moment when nations defined by language tried to establish and consolidate themselves in space and time. But it is also clear that the restrictions of linguistic diversity on which the classification of languages into changing languages is based are by themselves of the highest linguistic interest, even without any regard for the endeavours of the nineteenth century Europe. Thus for instance are the restrictions of the variety between English, especially its earlier stages, and German extremely relevant for anybody working with the two languages even if he has no connection with all the extralinguistic implications of Schlegel's and Grimm's description of English as a kind of "Deutsch".

In order to account for these linguistically relevant facts, an explicit theory of language change and linguistic relationship is needed. It must be constructed in order to allow us to store in a rational way all the relevant information about the restrictions on linguistic diversity. Since according to the premises of our linguistic theory, every linguistic change is a substitution of one language for another in a given community, the first step should be an investigation of the more general concept of language substitution. It is essential for this concept that it is determined by the relation of languages to a social community. The process involved is therefore extralinguistic.

Languages can be substituted not only in a community but also in a locality. Language change is then defined by the relation of language to space so that also in this case the concept involves an extralinguistic process. Very often language substitution is defined by the relation of languages to both social communities and space. In all these cases we have two languages and one of them is in use in one community and/or area at an earlier time while the other is used in the same community and/or area at a later time. This explicit statement makes it evident that the substitution of languages is nothing but a particular mapping of the linguistic variety set on time, space and society.

The linguistic variety set exists actually only in relation to the three sets of data which constitute the dimensions of a three-dimensional space. Every language is in use at a particular time, in a particular area and in a particular social community. The existence of a variety set of languages implies the variety of points in time, in space and of communities or of social settings. The common economy of efforts makes people avoid the use of two languages at the same time in the same area and in the same community and social setting. Therefore it can be stated quite generally that a change in language is always accompanied by a change in time and/or in space and/or in society. The converse is also true and it can be maintained that linguistic variety is a function of time variety and/or space variety and/or social variety. Changes in these three sets of data imply also changes in language. The substitution of languages in a place and/or a community is thus to be viewed as a part of a bigger complex of mapping relations.

According to the insights won in the nature of language substitution we shall introduce four sets. One of them is L, the linguistic variety set. Its members are all the languages that can be perceived as different:

$$= L \quad \{l_1, l_2, l_3 \ldots l_n\}.$$

This set is very large but not infinite. The second is the time set T, it contains all the time data connected with linguistic activity:

$$= T \quad \{t_1, t_2, t_3 \ldots t_m\}.$$

The space set S is the third. Its members are all the data about space connected with linguistic activity:

$$= S \quad \{s_1, s_2, s_3 \ldots s_p\}.$$

The fourth and last one is the community set C containing all the data about social communities and settings:

$$= C \quad \{c_1, c_2, c_3 \ldots c_q\}.$$

In all these sets the criteria for the identity of their members can be adjusted to our purposes and some perceivable differences can be disregarded. Thus we can introduce all dialects of English as one member of L, and all members of T can be centuries if we think it convenient. The whole territory of France can be a member of S and the population of the U.S.A. a member of C. But if they are useful, more subtle distinctions can always be made.

We introduce further three functions f, g and h. By f L is mapped on T, by g on S and by h on C.

It is possible now to state what language change means in the terms of the introduced sets and functions. Every language change is an ordered subset of L. Let us take the simplest case in which one language is substituted for another. We have then $\langle l_i \; l_j \rangle$ which is an ordered subset of L. If $\langle l_i \; l_j \rangle$ is a language change, it must fulfill the following conditions: f (l_i) and f (l_j) must not be equal; g (l_i) and g (l_j) and/or h (l_i) and h (l_j) must be equal. In symbolical notation this condition can be exposed as follows:

(1) $\wedge \neq f (l_i) f (l_j) \vee = g (l_i) g (l_j) = h (l_i) h (l_j).$

In other words, two languages constitute a language change if their f's are different and their g's and/or their h's the same. Language change is in this way defined by the mapping of L on T,

S and C. One of the three functions must be different while at least one of the two remaining must be the same. The discipline concerned with subsets of L so defined is historical linguistics.

It is readily seen that our condition for language change is only one of three possible ways to comply with the general requirement stated above. Not only f but also g and h can be the function of l_i and l_j that is obligatorily different, and it is then always possible for at least one of the two remaining functions to be the same.

One of the other possibilities to comply with the general requirement is:

$$(2) \quad \wedge \neq g\,(l_i)\ g\,(l_j)\ \vee\ =\ f\,(l_i)\ f\,(l_j)\ =\ h\,(l_i)\ h\,(l_j).$$

Here the g function is obligatorily unequal and at least one of the remaining two functions is obligatorily equal. The function g maps L on S. Every subset defined by (2) consists of languages spoken in different areas at the same time and/or in the same social community or setting. The linguistic disciplines concerned with such subsets of L are linguistic geography and dialectology.

The third possibility to comply with the general requirement is:

$$(3) \quad \wedge \neq h\,(l_i)\ h\,(l_j)\ \vee\ =\ f\,(l_i)\ f\,(l_j)\ =\ g\,(l_i)\ g\,(l_j).$$

Here the h function is obligatorily different and at least one of the two remaining functions is obligatorily equal for both languages. The discipline concerned with such subsets of L is linguistic sociology.

Historical linguistics, linguistic geography and the sociology of language are parts of the linguistic science each investigating a class of subsets of L. These classes are defined by (1), (2) and (3) respectively. The three disciplines exhaust logically all possibilities to classify languages in accordance to constants and variables in the three sets of extralinguistic data on which L is mapped.

The mapping of L on T, S and C is a general model of the relation of languages to the world in which they are spoken.[2] Languages are social institutions and they are always used in com-

---

[2] Cf. Katičić (1966a, 57 ff.).

munities which exist in a certain place at a certain time. The general model by making these relations explicit shows us that the differenciation between geographical and social dialects is a phenomenon of the same kind as language change. The deep logical affinity of linguistic geography and linguistic sociology with historical linguistics is not easily grasped by common sense. At first sight they seem to be two rather different things. One of the reasons for it may be the fact that the subsets of L selected by (1) are necessarily ordered while the subsets selected by (2) and (3) are not. This is intuitively evident, but if we investigate it further it becomes plain that the subsets selected by (1) are in themselves no more necessarily ordered than those selected by (2) and (3).

The subsets of L selected by (1) become ordered because the values of f for all members of L are ordered. This is so because T is by the very nature of time an ordered set. On the other hand, S and C can also be ordered if we choose to order them arbitrarily, whereas the ordering of T is given by the natural sequence of time units. The change subsets of L are ordered by the ordered values of f (l_i) and f (l_j) which are obligatorily different.

The subsets of L selected in a different way are therefore never labeled as 'language changes' although on second thought it is easy to understand that they are equally entitled to this label. There is no reason to deny that languages change when we move in space or in social strata, not less than they change when we shift our point in time. The difference that impresses itself on the common-sense observer is the natural orderedness of the subsets of L he is used to call language change as opposed to the unorderedness of the other subsets selected by their mapping on T, S and C. And yet, the basic affinity of language history with linguistic geography (dialectology) and linguistic sociology manifests itself very clearly in the traditional subjects of linguistic research. The replacement of Latin by Italian in familiar use in the communities of Italy can be viewed as a subject of both language history and linguistic sociology. The fact that Lithuanian is more conservative than Lettonian belongs to linguistic history and geography alike.

If we choose to order, in any arbitrary way, the members of

S and T, then the three extralinguistic sets form a three-dimensional space in which the members of L are located by the functions f, g, h. Fig. 1 shows how a language is located in the three-dimensional space defined by T, S and C.

Fig. 2 represents a change subset of L in which both g and h are

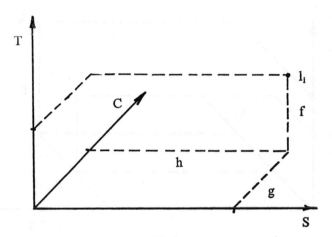

Fig. 1.

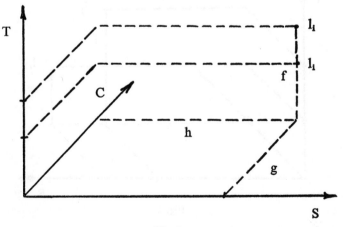

Fig. 2.

invariable, whereas fig. 3 and fig. 4 show them alternatively variable and invariable. These are the three types of mapping which comply with (1) and thus select change subsets of L.[3]

The selecting of geographical and sociological subsets of L by (2) and (3) can be presented in an analoguous manner.

Language change as defined by (1) is a very broad concept and

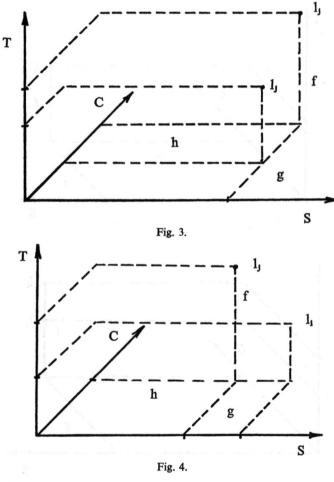

Fig. 3.

Fig. 4.

[3] Cf. Katičić (1966a, 57 ff.).

includes very different processes. Everything we are inclined to label as language change is comprized there together with other happenings we usually prefer to label only as substitution. Our concept includes *e.g.*, both the change from Ugro-Finnic to Russian which occurred in the region of Moscow and the substitution of New-High-German for Middle-High-German in Southern Germany. Only the second will readily be accepted as language change *i.e.*, as the changing of one language, whereas the first case will be considered as a change of the areas of two different languages, *i.e.*, as an expansion of Russian in a former Ugro-Finnic area. If an explanation is asked for this distinction, the answer will be that in the southern German case there is an inner relationship between the two languages, whereas in the case of Central Russia there is none. Therefore we shall adopt the terms 'internal' and 'external' language change' in order to denote the two different ways in which language change, as defined in our theory, can take place.

Although the common nature of external and internal language change is an important fact which our system of linguistic concepts has allowed us to discover, the difference between them is evident and it will be therefore profitable to try to express it in terms of our model. In what does the language substitution in Central Russia differ from the one in Southern Germany? And it must be stressed that they differ to the extent that linguists do not traditionally recognize the fundamental identity of both processes, but accept only the second as language change. The correct answer seems to be that Russian had already been used as a language in other regions and communities before it was substituted for Ugro-Finnic in the region of Moscow, whereas New-High-German had been used nowhere before it supplanted Middle-High-German in its area. This is, in terms of our model, the essential difference between the two classes of language substitution. Internal language change can now be defined as language change in which the later language never existed outside the area in which it substituted the earlier one. We can say that external change is a substitution of an imported language, whereas in internal change the later language grows spontaneously in the same area and/or in the same community in which the earlier was used.

This definition of internal change is not based on the 'inner relationship' existing between the earlier and later stage in internal language change. For the time being it is necessary to disregard this very important criterion because with the theoretical concepts introduced so far we are unable to take it into consideration. The members of the variety set L are defined only as non-identical and therefore, at this stage, internal language change cannot be defined by restrictions on their diversity since the degree of this diversity is yet irrelevant to our theory. But it is highly significant that even with the concepts now at our disposal we are able to define internal linguistic change as a language substitution with additional restrictions. This confirms the view that internal change is but a special case of language substitution.

The great achievement of the nineteenth century linguists was that they incorporated internal change into the identity criteria of languages. They proposed, in other words, to regard languages connected by internal change as different forms of one changing language. As a consequence of this linguistic theory such familiar statements as: "Italian and French are two modern forms of Latin" became possible. In older times, when Dante wrote his *De vulgari eloquentia* this proposition would have been accepted as nonsense because the linguistic theory which, implicitely at least, includes internal change into the criteria for the identity of a language was yet unknown.

An internal change is an ordered subset of L satisfying the conditions stated above. Such an ordered subset can have an unlimited number of members. They all together form the internal change. The membership in such an ordered internal change subset of L is called linguistic descent. Any member language is a descendant of the members preceding it in the ordered subset. Thus linguistic descent depends entirely on internal linguistic change.

Languages connected in any way by descent are said to be genetically related. This connection by descent may come about by membership in one and the same or in several intersecting internal change subsets of L. The second possibility of genetic relationship by membership in diverse but intersecting internal change subsets must be admitted because of the fact, well-known to comparativists, that a language may have more than one descendant which in their turn are not descendants of each other. The question, how internal change subsets can intersect, will be fully discussed in a subsequent chapter of this book.[4]

Perhaps it will be useful to add at this point a few words in order to prevent a misunderstanding that may otherwise eventually arise. It must be stressed that our general model of the relations of languages to the extralinguistic world and the definitions of internal and external language change are not being propounded as a device which will help us to recognize a linguistic change and to classify it as internal or external, but as a system of concepts which will help us to understand what such changes are. The purpose of the model as introduced here is not to provide a procedure which will make it possible to decide whether in a given case there is language change or not, and if there is, to qualify it as external or internal, but to offer a basis for an explicit definition of the important concept of language change.

Our model cannot be used for the discovery of genetic relationship among languages because of the impossibility to define in an exact way the communities that form C as its members. Still more difficult is the question of the identity of changing social communities. Did the citizens of London in the twelfth century form the same community as they do now? Thus in order to decide if in a given case there is a language change the much more arduous problem of social change and of the identity of changing communities must be previously solved if in the putative language change only the mapping of both languages on C is constant.

The data of time and space can be exactly expressed in years, decades and centuries or in geographical longitude and latitude. The identity of temporal and spacial data cannot present a prob-

[4] Cf. p. 146ff.

lem in the narrow frame in which the speech phenomenon occurs. Therefore it would be preferable to define the concept of linguistic change by the mapping of L on T and S only with the exclusion of C. But this is impossible since social communities may be relevant as constants in respect to which languages are substituted even if these communities change their habitats. If a language change, internal or external, takes place in a tribe on the wandering the social community is the only constant in respect to which there is a substitution of languages. For this reason the mapping of L on C cannot be disregarded. So our model can be useful only for the definition of language change, internal and external, but it cannot always help us to prove that a given ordered subset of L is or is not a language change.

There is one more reason for which it is difficult to use our model in order to recognize whether or not we have in a given case to do with language change and especially to discern internal from external change. To use the model in this way we need complete information and all the T, S and C data concerning the languages in question must be at our disposal. In actual fact this almost never happens. Therefore it would be very difficult to prove the existence of an internal change because in the terms of the model here proposed it is necessary to know almost everything about languages in order to be able to ascertain that a later language was used nowhere outside the area and/or the community in which it has supplanted an earlier one. So complete a knowledge about the use of languages in all the areas and in all the communities of the world at all times is never available.

In spite of this unavoidable uncertainty, we accept with no doubt the statement that Middle-English changed internally into Modern-English. But we accept this not on the evidence of the data contained in T, S and C but because the diversity between the languages is restricted in a certain way. We recognize internal change by the restriction of diversity between the languages that are its stages. These restrictions, ignored so far by our definitions, are thus of great importance. This again is a lesson taught by nineteenth century linguistics: Languages related genetically can be recognized as such by the restrictions imposed on their diversity. The method by which we achieve this is traditionally called the comparative method. So it is not extralinguistic but linguistic data that make it actually possible to recognize and to prove the existence of internal change and hence of linguistic descent and genetic relationship. To examine the way in which this can be brought about is the main purpose of this book.

But why, it may be asked, was it necessary to introduce the intricate model in which linguistic variety is mapped on sets of extralinguistic data? It could be argued that it is entirely superfluous to consider extralinguistic data when internal change can be recognized by the observations of restrictions imposed on linguistic diversity.

This objection raises the question of whether language change can be defined by linguistic concepts only. The answer to this question is in the negative. We need extralinguistic concepts in order to define language change and genetical relationship in linguistics. Internal change can be RECOGNIZED by restrictions imposed on linguistic diversity but it cannot be said TO BE itself such a restriction of the diversity of languages. At first sight it may seem attractive to define internal change by the procedure by which we discover it, but it is easy to demonstrate that what language change is should be distinguished from how it can be recognized and proved. This can be shown to be true by the well-known fact that there may be languages, related genetically, which cannot be recognized as such because the restrictions on their diversity have faded away in the course of a change with many replacements so that the observable restrictions are no more conclusive enough.

The question has been considered in linguistics whether Modern English and Modern Persian could be recognized as genetically related languages if only they were known of all the Indo-European family. Let us suppose for a moment that the answer to this question is in the negative. The two languages would none the less be genetically related. It follows that genetical relationship and hence linguistic descent and internal linguistic change can exist even if there are no conclusive restrictions imposed on the diversity of the languages under examination. Hence genetic relationship and linguistic descent on one side and the restrictions of linguistic diversity of which they are the cause and by which they are recognized on the other must be clearly distinguished. It is therefore impossible to define language change, linguistic descent and genetic relationship by linguistic concepts only.

Here the objection could be raised that if two languages are genetically related and they do not show it by the restrictions of their diversity, then a certain number of languages, attested or not, must exist that can be arranged in such a string that every two languages placed in it next to one another present all the restrictions of diversity that are necessary in order to qualify the languages as being one the descendant of the other and hence genetically related. In this way even such cases as that of English and Persian could be accounted for by a concept of genetic relationship, defined as a certain kind of mediated restriction imposed on linguistic diversity. It would then again be unnecessary to define genetic relationship by resorting to extralinguistic concepts.

Against this objection two things can be said. Such a definition does not, in the first place, make it possible to handle the concept of genetic relationship in any practical way. It supposes linguistic data we may not have at our disposal in every case. In this respect it is no better than the definition based on T, S, C data as was proposed above. It can only be contended that it is theoretically neater because it does not involve extralinguistic concepts and that it should be preferred on this ground. But such a contention is not proof against further analysis. A very simple mental experiment can show this. If two languages by pure coincidence exhibit restrictions of diversity characteristic of genetic relationship we shall still not be able to say that they are genetically related. This is so because the establishment of genetic relationship between two languages is a statement about what happened in the past and not about the present state of things. What happened in the past can best be recognized and proved by the present state of things but it is not the present state itself. Therefore genetic relationship cannot be defined as a special case of restriction of linguistic diversity. Such a definition is not defendable theoretically and the mapping of linguistic variety on extralinguistic data is needed in order to define language change, linguistic descent and genetic relationship of languages.

By accepting the proposed definition of language change and the others deduced from it the problem of genetic relationship which is central in comparative linguistics is not yet solved but only stated in a clear way. The methodological task presented by research in comparative linguistics can now be explicitly formulated. Languages themselves are, as far as linguistic data go, nothing but a variety with some restrictions imposed on their diversity. In connection with time, space, and social communities, subsets of the linguistic variety set can be selected. In accordance with the requirements they comply with they can be qualified as subsets of external and internal change and as classes of genetically related languages. But we do not have at our disposal all the necessary information about the connection of the various languages with time, space and social communities and so it is unpracticable for us to select the subsets by the very functions that define them. We must try to find other means to select these subsets.

It can be easily observed that languages entering in the same change subset exhibit a restricted diversity. This restricted diversity may help us to find out to what change subset a given language belongs. This is the course adopted by comparative linguistics. It classifies languages in accordance with their genetic relationship as shown by their restricted diversity. This task is made more difficult by our uncomplete knowledge of L. We can never be sure that no member of the selected change subset remains unknown to us. Such missing links, if their number is great, can make it impossible for us to recognize languages that should by our criteria enter into a selected subset. Therefore one is never sure that research work in comparative linguistics will be crowned with success and it can never be proven that any given languages are not related genetically.

Language change has been shown to include a very wide range

of phenomena which are almost never brought under one label by common sense. It was therefore necessary to distinguish between external and internal language change. Now we shall investigate how this two kinds of language change affect the diversity of the linguistic variety set.

External change, as defined above, is a special case of a more general phenomenon which is accounted for by the broad concept of language contact. The replacement of one language by another brings about a very close contact between the two languages. It happens then what is expected to happen when languages come in close contact — they show a marked tendency to develop loan correspondences and to become thus languages related by loan. This means that languages involved in external change are each for themselves subject to internal change in such a way that the descendant languages in the internal changes are related by loan whereas the earlier languages were not or were so in a lesser degree.

Loan relationship can thus in certain cases remain as a trace of external change: the languages involved in it will take loanwords from each other and they will show an increase of typological correspondences. These linguistic traces of external language change are not specific and systematic enough to serve as a basis for a strict demonstration of the fact that two languages were involved in such a change, but they can be recognized and thoroughly observed. The linguistic consequences of external change are well known in linguistics under the name of 'substratum influences' and linguists were at times very hopeful about the possibility of explaining internal change and genetic relationship by them.

Here, two different opinions have to be distinguished. According to one of them, the restrictions imposed on linguistic diversity which are traditionally regarded as the consequence of genetic relationship, are nothing but very marked instances of loan relationship and can therefore be entirely accounted for by loan words and typological correspondences. In the light of such a view, what is usually assumed to be genetic relationship is in fact nothing but loan relationship and differs from the other cases of loan relationship only in degree. If this is true, languages that are currently considered as genetically related are in fact only very closely related by loan. So those linguists who are prone to explain genetic relationship as a kind of loan relationship must admit a very considerable difference in degree where others see a difference in kind.[5]

According to the other view, internal change is a consequence of language contact and especially of external change. If this is true, a language changes with the influences it undergoes in contact with other languages. This is the explanation of internal language chance by substratum and adstratum influences which has been repeatedly tried but never with complete success. Genetic relationship would come about by the differentiations of a language which develops loan correspondences with various other languages. Such an assumption by which 'language mixing' is the moving force of internal language change cannot easily be accepted as a correct explanation since nobody has succeeded so far in establishing one-to-one relations between internal change and the traces of external change and other forms of linguistic contact. A great deal of internal change can eventually be explained that way but not the whole of it. It would be perhaps nearer to the truth to contend that internal change is not caused by contact with other languages but that it can be influenced by it as far as the direction it takes is concerned. English has not changed because it came in close contact with Norman French, a contact which amounts to partial external change, but, while changing, it was in many details of its change influenced by this contact.

Though external change cannot be strictly proved by the loan relationship it establishes between languages, it is in most cases not very difficult to recognize its traces on languages that have undergone it. The extralinguistic evidence that is necessary in order to establish an external change is also generally available.

Things are very different with internal change. Here we must know whether the new language has been in use somewhere else before it has replaced the earlier one. Such a complete knowledge

---

[5]   Cf. Trubeckoj (1939) where this approach finds its classical expression.

of extralinguistic data is almost never at our disposal. Internal change and consequently linguistic descent and genetic relationship can be traced and proved only by their effects on the languages that are involved in the internal changes in question. Fortunately, these effects are more extensive and much more systematic than it is the case with mere substratum influence.

The recognizable trace that internal change leaves on the languages is brought about by the regularity of sound change which was observed by the *Junggrammatiker* in the sixties and seventies of the last century. They had based on this regularity their concept of sound law which caused at that time a heated controversy.

The idea of reducing genetical to loan relationship has undoubtedly a sound core because both external and internal change are language substitution and thus subclasses of one and the same class of processes. Our theory accounts for this fact by introducing one general concept of language change.[6] But our theory distinguishes also between external and internal change and in doing so it keeps the opposition between genetic and loan relationship as different not in degree but in kind. The full justification of this decision must be reserved for the chapter on the genetic classification of languages. For the time being, it will suffice to point out that external change is at least in one respect radically different from internal. Whereas internal change tends to diminish the typological relationship of the languages involved, English and Indoarian are very impressive examples of this tendency, external change is bound to augment it in the course of time as the balkanic and caucasic languages clearly show.

---

[6]   The same content is given to the term "language change" by Hoenigswald (1960, 22 and 28).

4

THE REGULARITY OF SOUND CHANGE

Internal change has been defined as a spontaneous replacement of a language by another which has previously not been in use outside the community and/or the area of the replaced one. The crucial question is now whether anything can be said about the relations that can be expected to exist between replacing and the replaced language.

It is a basic empirical fact that in every community and/or in every area for some unknown and at this moment irrelevant reasons new languages are being spontaneously introduced without any external influence. This is probably a consequence of the unability of human beings to keep their speech performances constantly up to a most complex pattern. Therefore it becomes exceedingly difficult to recall at any moment all the details of a language. The only source of information about language are the actual performances of the speakers, and as they conform only to a varying degree to the requirements of the language, essential information about its patterns may be lost in the process.[1]

When such a new language is introduced, two things can happen to it. It may remain an individual trait in the speach of one speaker or it may spread by imitation and replace the older language in an area or in a community or in both. Only if the later happens will the replacement be registered as language change. If the new language remains individual, it will disappear at latest with the

---

[1] About the causes of spontaneous language change and especially of spontaneous sound change cf. Martinet (1955, 47 ff. and 1961, 177 ff.), Hockett (1958, 439 ff.), Gleason (1965, 394 f.)

person that introduced it and will thus remain unnoticed and irrelevant for language history. Both possibilities are open for
every new language introduced spontaneously, but it is reasonable
to assume that it does not depend only on pure chance whether
such a new language will spread or not. To a certain extent it
must depend on the inherent properties of the new language and
especially on its relations to the language it replaces. For one,
there is the necessity to maintain the possibility of communication
between the speakers of the old and the speakers of the new language during the process of replacement which it may take many
years to achieve fully. This necessity imposes very serious restrictions on the choice of successful spontaneous replacements.[2]
This choice is thus limited only to such languages which are in-
telligible without difficulties to the speakers of the older language.

The spreading of the new language is in the case of internal
change deprived of the support of any external factor providing
an incentive for the speakers of the older language to make an
effort in order to understand the new one. It is always such an
incentive that makes external change possible. And it is an extralinguistic situation which provides the incentive. The extralinguistic situation is in its turn connected with the community and/or
the area in which the new language was in use before it began
to replace the older language. So the whole mechanism presupposes the conditions of external change and hence it cannot operate
in internal change, where by definition the new language was never
spoken before in another community and/or in another area.

The new language has in internal change no outward support.
The speakers of the replaced language have no reason whatsoever
to make a special effort in order to understand it. It is therefore
very probable that in internal change the successful replacing languages will be in such a relation to the replaced ones that makes
the transcoding from one into the other easy. But it is important
to note that facility of transcoding from the old language into the
new one is more important than the reverse. For the speakers of

---

[2] Cf. Dyen (1963).

the old language must accept the new one if it is to spread, whereas the speakers of the new language either know the old one and have since no difficulties in transcoding or they ignore it and have thus no need of transcoding. Thus when in internal change Indo-European *dh* was in early Iranian identified with *d* it was necessary for the speakers of the older language to know how to transform all phonemic strings containing a *dh* while the speakers of the successfully spreading new language either knew where the *dh*'s were in the phonemic strings of the older language or they did not use the older language at all and went on confounding *d* and *dh* in all situations. Even so texts of the older language remained understandable to the speakers of the new one, only they did not imitate them any more.

If the double articulation of language into morphemes and phonemes is not only a convenient device for the description of speech, but corresponds in some way to the real processes by which the speakers' activity is performed, facility of transcoding can be stated in terms of items of language structure.[3] As a broad generalization it can be said that transcoding will be easier if the correspondence relations between the older and the new language can be expressed as a correspondence of distribution statable in terms of linguistic units only with no additional information. From this and from what was said before it can be deduced that the relations between the successfully replacing and the replaced language will in the vast majority of cases be such that correspondence relations can be stated in terms of linguistic units. This is to say that the correspondence relations between strings of units will have a high degree of regularity.

Furthermore, as the transcoding of their language into a new language must be especially easy for the speakers of the older one if the new one is to be successful, in the vast majority of cases this correspondence will be strictly predictable for every unit in every environment of units of the same rank in the older language. The same is not true for all the units in all environments of the new language. This can be expected because there is no other way to

[3]   Cf. Martinet (1960, 19).

make the transcoding easier for the speakers of the older language. In such a case they have only to learn how every already well known unit in a given environment has to be replaced in order to obtain a string of units belonging to the new language. The same would be of little use to the speakers of the new language since they either know the old language or do not use it.

From this general reasoning only a statistical tendency of successful new languages can be deduced, rather than a law without exceptions. In any case we can be sure that the successful new languages (and only they are relevant here) will show a neat tendency toward one-many correspondences between their units and those of the older language. Only so the replacement of units can be predictable. This is the principle of regularity in internal change.

By virtue of this principle, the phonemic correspondences between replaced and replacing language gain a particular significance. The phonemic system of a language provides a device which makes it possible to express the contents of all morphemes with a small number of units recurring frequently in various morphs. Morph we shall call here the strings of phonemes that serve as the expression of morphemic contents. Morpheme, on the other hand, denotes the whole complex unit with one or more expressions (allomorphs) and a content attached to them.

The frequency of recurrence of the phonemes in morphs makes their correspondence relations extremely conspicuous. And in accordance with the principle of regularity the morphs of the new language will be predictable given the morphs of the older one with a set of one-valued replacement rules. Thus the relation between the morphs of the two languages will be very regularly patterned. As mutual intelligibility must be preserved in every single replacement, the phonetic substance in which the replacing phonemes are realized cannot be very different from the substance in which the replaced phonemes were realized. Most conspicuous is the regularity of sound replacement. It is thanks to it in the first place that the occurrence of internal change can be established by linguistic data only.

This can be achieved if the statistical tendency towards regularity is taken as the basis of the description of phonemic replacement or sound change, as it is called more traditionally. For that purpose it is most convenient to assume that this tendency is a strict law to which sound change always conforms but which is often successfully counteracted by other factors which are themselves, at least in principle, also objectively controlable. This assumption was first made by the *Junggrammatiker* in the seventies of the last century and remains since then hotly disputed.[4] The immediate result of this assumption was an overwhelming progress in the understanding of language phenomena and especially of language history.

But while making the assumption of regular sound change[5] and gathering its rich harvest, the *Junggrammatiker* and their followers were not aware of the true epistemological nature of their new concept of sound law. They introduced it as a description of immediate reality, and it was therefore much criticized from the very beginning. Very soon it was even proven to be wrong by linguistic geography. The search of a boundary between the high and the low german dialects revealed a fan of unexpectedly individual isoglosses instead of the sharp boundary expected in accordance with the notion of regular sound change.[6] Further research made it clear that no corpus of significant extent complies fully with the requirement of sound laws. The morphs of no language can in their entirety be derived from the morphs of another by single-valued replacement rules stated in terms of phonemes and phoneme environments. The assumption of regularity of sound change is in this sense untenable. It is certainly not the faithful description of an immediately given reality.

But while claiming that sound laws are exceptionless, the *Junggrammatiker* provided in their very theory a place for exceptions

---

[4] Cf. Osthoff-Brugmann (1878), Paul (1909, 67 ff.), Schuchardt (1885). In recent times new insights have been gained into the nature of sound change and into the causes of its being regular. Cf. Hoenigswald (1960, 72 ff. and 1964), Fourquet (1964), Ladd (1964), Gleason (1965, 395), Hockett (1965, 200 ff.).

[5] Cf. Hockett (1965, 186 ff.).

[6] Cf. Wenker (1881, etc.) and Wenker-Wrede (1895, etc.).

by introducing the concepts of analogy, dialect borrowing and individual sound change due to assimilation, dissimilation, haplology, paretymology, etc. This means that in practice there will never be a corpus whose morphs show exclusively such a distribution of phonemes as can be predicted on the basis of established sound laws. The assumption of regular sound change does not claim that the real effects of internal change conform absolutely to sound laws, but only that they would do so if the sound laws were not counteracted by other factors. As the latter is always the case, what is really found is only a more or less neat tendency towards such regularity, a tendency that, as we believe to have shown, in circumstances of internal change must be expected.

This assumption of a regularity which manifests itself fully only if all other factors are excluded is a familiar one and it occurs often in science. A body, once put in motion will continue to move indefinitely, but it never does because of other factors, disregarded in the general statement, but always present in reality. A feather and a stone would, as to gravity, fall alike, if it were not for other factors preventing the full realization of this tendency. In all these cases a very complex reality is represented as the result of conflicting tendencies. Each of them is postulated as absolute and exclusive but impaired in its effects by opposing influences. The complex reality is thus described in terms of conflicting tendencies every one of which is in itself absolutely regular and has predictable effects. The difference between sound laws and the laws of nature is not as great, after all, as has often been argued and is generally believed.

The most significant difference between them is that the sound laws are limited in space and time whereas the laws of nature are not. But this is true only for the single phoneme replacement rules and not for the regularity of sound replacement as such. And it is only the latter that can, in any serious way, be regarded as an analogue to the laws of nature. This regularity is in internal language change as universal as any law of nature can ever be, for it is a necessary consequence of the very circumstances under which internal change is coming about.

The factors preventing the full realization of the regularity of sound change must, of course, be also strictly formulated and made predictable. And, at least in principle, they are. The fact that many linguists have sinned by abuse of analogical explanations by no means invalidates the basic requirement that for every assumed analogical readjustment the conditioning morphological patterns should be established. So, for instance, to say that the plural form of *book*, predictable by the phonemic replacement rules as *beech*, has been analogically replaced by *books* is no gratuitous assertion but can be substantiated by the existence of a pattern of plural formation of substantives with an overwhelming frequent occurrence.

In the example given here the validity of the analogical explanation is evident. In fact, it is a question of probability and information. If the plural forms of all English substantives except *book* are known, and if we try to guess the plural form of *book*, then *books* is much more probable than *beech* and conveys hence much less information. Generally, it can be said that a form unpredictable by regular phoneme replacement rules can be accounted for by analogy only if it is possible to show that among other forms with a corresponding content it is more probable and gives hence less information than the expected one. The more so, the less disputable is the analogical explanation. Analogical change tends thus to lessen the information conveyed by the construction of forms. In doing so it improves language communication, since information about the code is noise from the point of view of language communication. The less we learn from a speech performance about the speaker's language the better we understand his message. So in every case where analogical change is assumed it must be shown how it diminishes code information.

In a similar way the conditions can be stated under which an explanation by individual sound adjustment (assimilation, dissimilation, haplology, etc.) can be accepted. Here it is the informativity or redundancy of phonemic distinctive features which is increased or diminished in a phonemic string.

The chief weakness of all these explanations consists in the fact

that it remains impossible to predict which of the described tendencies will prevail in every given case. This cannot be otherwise
because we are yet unable to measure in any objective way their
respective strength nor do we know how strong analogy must be
in order to alter the effects of regular sound change. But it must
be said, that the main purpose of the theory of sound laws is not
to predict change, which would be a quite absurd endeavour with
the means we have at our disposal, but to account for the state
of the language of a given corpus.

Whereas analogy and individual sound adjustments are fully
accountable as to the conditions under which they occur, dialect
borrowing is the most freely manipulated of all tendencies counter-
acting regular sound change that were mentioned above. This is
so because the dialect from which forms are borrowed may and
may not be known from a corpus of texts. This means that whenever forms coexisting in a language can be derived from the forms
of the older language by regular but conflicting rules for the replacement of phonemes, dialect borrowing can be assumed, regardless to whether such a dialect is attested elswhere or not. A
language (or a dialect) is genetically defined by a set of sound laws
deriving its phonemic strings from an older language whose descendant the younger one is. Wherever two mutually exclusive
sound laws can be stated, we have to do with two languages regardless of the underlying speech realities. When in classical Sanscrit
i.-e., *l* is once changed in *r* and in other cases in *l* without any conditioning surroundings, then we must conclude that in the Sanscrit
texts there are two Old-Indian dialects regardless of whether such
dialects are known from other texts, regardless even of whether
they were ever used in any community.

This is the price we must pay in order to maintain the postulate
of exceptionless sound laws. If in a given internal change there
happened to be two points of crystallization for the necessary tendency towards regular many-one correspondences in phoneme
replacements, we shall say that the older language was replaced
by two new languages (dialects), that they borrowed from each
other and that one of them went out of use whereas the other

remained with borrowings from the lost language (dialect). In this way even very complex real processes in language change can be adequately described without abandoning the assumption of regularity of sound change. This is in full accordance with the general tendency towards regularity which is necessarily present in internal language change. This tendency allows us to recognize the effects of internal language change even without any extra-linguistic data for its establishment. And it was precisely in order to achieve this that the regularity assumption has been introduced. After internal change has been so redefined by regularity, every regular change that can be established determines a particular language (dialect) while all data concerning extralinguistic reality remain irrelevant in this respect.

The regularity assumption which postulates exceptionless sound laws is a theory deduced from the fundamental properties of internal language change intended to describe a very complex reality as the effect of clearly definable and conflicting tendencies. By reducing complexity to simplicity and stressing recurrence in variety it allows us to establish internal change by linguistic data alone. The success it had in this respect from its first formulation up to the present justifies it amply in spite of all its weaknesses and it is worth while to try to understand its fundamental properties and to see what its limitations and the prospects of further improvement are.

The notion of phonemic replacement rules suggests immediately transformations as known in cybernetics.[7] But the applicability of this flexible concept to our subject is much broader. It is essential to point out that linguistic variety itself can be presented as a set of cybernetic transformations. Let the linguistic variety set L be composed of n members, being a noticeably different language each:

$$= L \{l_1, l_2, l_3 \ldots l_n\}$$

Linguistic variety is presented here in terms of the set theory. An equivalent presentation can be given in terms of cybernetic trans-

[7]   Cf. Ross Ashby (1953, 9 ff.).

formations if we take, say, l_1 as an operand and apply to it a set of operators:

$$\{v_{1,2} \ v_{1,3} \ v_{1,4} \ \cdots \ v_{1,n}\}$$

which transform it into l_2, l_3, l_4 ... l_n respectively. We can generally say that the diversity of any two members of L can be expressed by an operator transforming the one into the other:

$$v_{i,j} \ \Big\downarrow \ \begin{matrix} l_i \\ l_j \end{matrix}$$

Any member of the variety set can thus be alternatively conceived as an operand and as a transform. The variety set is thus reduced to an operand and a set of operators. Their number equates all the nonidentical dyads of the n members of L *i.e.* $\dfrac{n\,(n-1)}{1\,.\,2}$.

Although this presentation is equivalent to the other, it differs from it in a respect which is essential for our purposes. Whereas the statement in terms of the set theory contains independent descriptive models of all languages in the variety set and expresses thus their diversity only implicitly, the presentation in terms of transformations states the degree of diversity between any pair of languages in the variety set with full explicitness. The operators transforming any member of the variety set in all others describe the correspondence relations whereas in the other presentation these relations must be derived from the parallel descriptive models. Because of this property the transformational statement of linguistic variety deserves our closer attention for it can help us to understand better the nature of the regularity assumption as discussed above.

In our first sketch of a transformational presentation of linguistic variety, languages were regarded as indivisible wholes and the operators applied to them as such. In the case of

$$v_{i,j} \ \Big\downarrow \ \begin{matrix} l_i \\ l_j \end{matrix}$$

$v_{i,j}$ was supposed to apply to l_i as a whole and to transform it into l_j. But language is a complex structure and the operator can be formulated for each of the terms of its model apart. In such a case, because of the existence of linguistic universals, a part of the rules which constitute the operator will always be rules for identical transformations in which the operand and the transform are identical.

The model of any language consists from this point of view of two parts: the universals and the particular traits of the language in question. If we take u to symbolize the universals and p to symbolize the particular traits, our two languages l_i and l_j can be presented as $\{u, p_i\}$ and $\{u, p_j\}$. In such a case the operator $v_{i,j}: \rightarrow l_i \, l_j$ will consist of two rules, one of which will formulate an identical transformation:

$$v_{i,j}: \rightarrow p_i \; p_j$$
$$\rightarrow u \;\; u$$

The transformation itself becomes then twofold:

$$v_{i,j} \quad \Big\downarrow \quad \begin{array}{l} p_i \; u \\ p_j \; u \end{array}$$

If it happens that l_i and l_j are languages with a restricted diversity, *i.e.*, related languages in the broadest sense defined in chapter 2, then more rules than those concerning the universals will express identical transformations. Let r symbolize the part of the models of l_i and l_j where diversity is restricted. One rule must now be added to our statement of the operator $v_{i,j}$:

$$v_{i,j}: \rightarrow p_i \; p_j$$
$$\rightarrow r \;\; r$$
$$\rightarrow u \;\; u$$

and the transformation itself becomes threefold:

$$v_{i,j} \quad \Big\downarrow \quad \begin{array}{l} p_i \; r \; u \\ p_j \; r \; u \end{array}$$

This is the way in which the operators v explicitly express the kind and the degree of diversity between the members of L. All the restrictions of diversity will become visible as identical transformations beyond the universals.

In internal change the diversity between the replaced and the replacing language must be reduced to the extreme for the reasons discussed above. Mutual intelligibility will by necessity be preserved, and this can happen only if the r-part of the languages is very substantial. One typical case would be that in which the whole syntax (including morphology) and semantics (*i.e.*, the content of lexical morphemes) is transformed in identical transformations and remains thus unchanged from replaced to replacing language and the only non-identical transformations appear in the phonological component where the rules generating the expression of all morphemes are transformed so as to generate different though by necessity recognizable strings of phonemes. The assumption of regularity of phonemic replacement in internal language change presupposes in fact such a transformation.

Of course, phonemic replacements are not the only non-identical transformations occurring between older and new languages in internal change. There are also analogical redistributions and other changes in the distribution of morphs and in syntactic structure. But all these are increases of diversity which are independent of and irrelevant to the replacements of phonemes in morphs and they tend rather to obscure the conditions under which the phonemes were replaced. Thus in Greek an older language with *q* in certain morphs was succeeded by a new one in which this *q*, when before *e* and *i*, was replaced by *t* and elsewhere by *p*. So **qisis* became τίσις 'retribution' and **qoinā* ποινά 'blood money'. In the same way **leiqō* became λείπω 'I leave' and **leiqete* became **λείτετε* 'you leave'. But afterwards the morph λειπ was redistributed by analogy and prevailed in the whole paradigm. Since then the conditions in which *q* was replaced by *p* and *t* cannot any more be simply read from their actual distribution but they must be inferred from such examples as τίσις and ποινά, τίς 'who' and πότερος 'which one of two', where the morphs alternate in derivation and not in inflexions and are hence less exposed to analogical readjustments. The theory of regular sound replacement takes it thus implicitly for granted that while phonemic entities are being changed all other parts of the model of the older language are being replaced with identically transformed items. This assumption is in so far realistic as all non-phonemic replacements are irrelevant to sound change.

In some cases we must admit a probable connection between syntactic (including morphology) and phonological replacements. Thus for instance the replacement of final syllables with zero has undoubtedly something to do with the loss of grammatical categories and of the free word order though it is difficult to say which in this instance is the cause and which the effect. Whatever here the causal connection may be, the phonemic replacements are quite independent as to their own nature, for they can be stated independently, without any reference to the morphological and syntactic replacements.

In this sense it can be assumed that the non-identical replacement of phonemes goes always with an identical transformation of all other items of the model. In other words, wherever there is internal language change there will be also identical replacements of language units except for the phonemic expression of morphemes.

In such instances everything except the replacements of phonemes in morphs will be accounted for by the identical transformations $\rightarrow$ u u and $\rightarrow$ r r and the third part of the transformation with the operator $\rightarrow$ p_i p_j will apply exclusively to phonemes as ordered in the morphs of the older language. This we can note by substituting ph to p and thus writing $\rightarrow$ ph_i ph_j.

The assumption of regularity in sound change can now be formulated as a specific formal property of the operator $\rightarrow$ ph_i ph_j. This operator will be a set of rules applying to the morphs of the older language (l_i). These rules will on their left side, i.e., on the side of ph_i, have only phonemes in phonemic environment. No non-phonological information will be needed for the identification of the items on the left side of the operator rules. Since phonemes specified by their phonemic environment are allophones, it can be said that on the left side of the → ph_i ph_j rules there will be only allophones and nothing else. In this way the rank of the units to which the operator of sound change is applied can be defined very precisely.

The fact that regular sound change is applied to allophones and not to phonemes supports the view held in generative phonology according to which a consistent presentation of the morphs is desirable only at the level of allophones (systematic phonetics) and not on that of phonemes (taxonomic phonemics).[8] For the statement of sound substitution in internal language change just as for the generative description of languages the allomorphic and not the phonemic presentation of morphs is necessary and most economic.

There is one more restriction imposed on the operator of regular sound change. According to the assumption of regularity, no disjunction is allowed on the right side of the rules. The operator of sound change can contain only one-one or many-one but no one-many transformation rules. This means that all rules containing a disjunction on their right side as e.g.,

$$→ a \underline{v} b c$$

are excluded from the sound change operators. Excluded by the first restriction are also all rules containing any non-phonemic information on their left side as e.g.,

$$→ t \ /\text{in verbs}/ \quad d.$$

The assumption of regularity of sound change amounts, in other words to the prediction that all disjunctions on the right side of the rules stating sound change can be eliminated by specifying phonologically the items (allophones) to which the operator is applied. This prediction expresses a statistical tendency which for reasons discussed above is extremely likely to determinate the distribution of phonemic entities in the morphs of two languages in the same line of descent. All cases which cannot be accounted for by such

---

[8] Cf. Chomsky (1964, 65 ff. especially 76) and Šaumjan (1962, 40).

rules will not be recognized as the effect of internal sound change and are to be explained by other means. Analogy, individual sound adjustment and dialect borrowing are most likely to furnish an explanation. If they do not, the case remains unexplained and can invalidate neither the regularity assumption nor the criteria by which the other explanations are admitted. Given the *a priori* character of the assumption, this is easy to understand. Such residual cases are a permanent challenge for the investigators to try by further phonemic specification or by a general restatement of the operator of sound change to integrate them into the operator or to find data by which one of the other explanations may become possible.

Because of the regularity of sound change the distribution of phonological entities in the strings of the replacing language is strictly determined by their distribution in the strings of the replaced one. If one language is in two internal changes replaced by two different new languages, there will be two different distributions, both determined by one and the same distribution in the replaced language. Accordingly, there will be recurring correspondence among phonological entities which form the morphs of languages connected by one and the same internal change or of such which belong to different ones sharing a common starting point because all of them start with the replacement of one and the same language. These correspondence relations allow to establish the effects of regular sound change and to determine in this way which languages belong to a line of descent in internal change or to different lines with a common starting point. In other words, recurrent correspondences of phonological entities are a thoroughly perceptible trace of internal change and can thus serve for the establishment of genetical relationship as defined by internal linguistic change in the foregoing chapter. These are precisely the correspondences that reduce linguistic diversity in a way characteristic for genetic relationship.[9] When languages have their diversity restricted by such correspondences a common origin can be inferred from their existence.

[9] Cf. chapter 2.

The correlation between internal linguistic change and regular sound replacement allows us to redefine internal change in purely linguistic terms. We can now say that internal change is such a linguistic change in which the distributions of phonemes in both replaced and replacing languages can be correlated by an operator conforming to the requirements stated above. If this definition is accepted, the notion of internal change does no more depend on data which in most cases must remain by necessity unknown.

It is, however, essential for language history that such a relation between languages can be strictly correlated to a specific process of language replacement that can well be defined by extralinguistic notions although its practical establishment on that basis may be difficult or even impossible. To disregard this would mean to renounce the understanding of internal language change as a part of human history to which it undoubtedly belongs. More than that, it would deprive us of the possibility of understanding the very nature of the regularity assumption, for it can be deduced only from the concept of internal change as defined extralinguistically. Only so it can be seen that regular replacement of allophones is what is most likely to happen under the stated extralinguistic conditions.

Nothing has been said so far about the causes and mechanisms of sound change. It seems that it is due to a slow but steady alteration of the phonetic realization of phonemes. This constant subphonemic change is probably caused by the fact that the optimal realization of phonemes at which the speakers aim is determined by the distribution of frequency of all recalled previous realizations and is thus not apt to remain stable for a longer time span since only a limited number of realizations can be recalled.[10]

It has been proposed to simplify the model of the mechanisms of internal language change by reducing sound change to dialect borrowing. The effect of total morph replacement by borrowing from a subphonemically different dialect would be a change of certain positional allophones of certain phonemes into other existing phones in all the forms in which those positional allo-

[10] Cf. Martinet (1955, 48 ff.), Hockett (1958, 440 ff. and 1965).

phones occur. The effect would be equivalent to what is generally thought to be regular sound change. Sound change can thus be regarded as a result of a contact of different dialects in one and the same speech community. Its mechanics is fundamentally that of borrowing with sound substitution.[11]

This idea is very attractive for its simplicity but it leaves un-explained how such closely related dialects with only subphonemic diversity come into existence if not through divergent sound change during a short time span and without total break of com-munication. And so it is again necessary to assume spontaneous sound change in order to explain the situation in which dialect borrowing of the sort discussed above can be assumed. It is true that we are unable to distinguish the effects of genuine spontaneous sound change from total morph replacement by borrowing from a closely related dialect. Therefore we describe the results of a process of language change in which both occurred *a posteriori* as spontaneous sound change alone.

Every genuine spontaneous sound change leads to the establish-ment of dialect variety in a speech community since it never does happen in the language of all the members of the community. Dialect borrowing becomes then very frequent and at the end it is impossible to tell which of the observed changes are due to sound change and which to borrowing since they all conform with the regularity assumption. Therefore the term regular sound change as we use it, applies to the combined effects of both mech-anisms.

There is a close parallel to this in the relation of internal to external language change. Whenever a language which has not been introduced from somewhere else replaces another in an area and/or in a community, we call such a replacement an internal change. In reality, the change is internal only for those localities and/or subcommunities, if not individuals, where the new language has replaced the older one quite spontaneously. For the rest of the area and/or of the community the change is in fact external.

[11]   Cf. Hoenigswald (1960b, 54f.).

But we qualify it nevertheless as internal since its effects are un-distinguishable from those of genuinely internal change. We even cannot tell where the change actually began and is thus really internal.

In every internal language change and hence in every sponta-neous sound change there is thus a good deal of dialect borrowing that cannot be identified. Many of such closely related dialects appear and disappear again during the process of replacement in a given area or a given community or both. This accounts well for the fact that sound replacement in internal language change, while tending to regularity, often presents some exceptions which are usually regular in themselves.

But the whole difficult question about the nature and the causes of spontaneous and regular sound change is irrelevant to the theoretical foundations of comparative linguistics. For that pur-pose the correlation between regular sound change, whatever its nature, and internal language change by which genetical relation-ship can be established is the only thing that matters. For the es-tablishment of genetical relationship becomes thus possible by tracing the effects of regular sound change and determining its direction.

It is easy to see that the application of operators modelling regular sound change leads to the establishment of specific corre-spondence relations among the phonemic strings that serve as operands and their transforms. Let us for example take the Proto-Slavic words: *rǫka* 'hand', *mǫka* 'torment', *mǫžь* 'man', *žena* 'woman', *med'a* 'border'. If we apply to them the operator

→ a	a		→ k	k
→ e	e		→ m	m
→ ǫ	u		→ n	n
→ ь	Ø		→ r	r
→ d'	đ		→ ž	ž
		→ "x"	"x"	(the transformation of the content is always an iden-tical one)

transforming them into of Serbo-Croatian words the transforms will be: *ruka* 'hand', *muka* 'torment', *muž* 'man', *žena* 'woman', *međa* 'border'.

By the application of the operator very definite correspondence relations have been created between the Proto-Slavic and the Serbo-Croatian words. The resulting correspondences of content are best described in terms of translatability, *i.e.*, by the statement that Proto-Slavic *rǫka* is supposed to be best translated by Serbo-Croatian *ruka* and so on. The correspondence of expression is in its turn best described in terms of phonemes specified as to their places in strings. The correspondence relation between the Proto-Slavic and Serbo-Croatian words in our example can thus be stated as the correspondence of *r:r, ǫ:u, k:k, a:a, m:m, ž:ž, ь:Ø, e:e, n:n, đ:d*. The recurrence of such phonemic correspondences necessarily increases with the number of strings (in our case of words) to which the transformation is applied. In the complete vocabulary of two languages this recurrence will be very marked. The recurrence of a correspondence is determined by the frequency of the corresponding phonemes.

If we apply now to the same Proto-Slavic words another operator:

→ a	a		→ k	k
→ ǫ	o		→ m	m
→ ь	Ø		→ n	n
→ đ	j		→ r	r
→ e	e		→ ž /not before ь/	ž
	→ ž / before ь/	š		
	→ "x"	"x"		

transforming them into Slovene words, the transforms will be *roka* 'hand', *moka* 'torment', *moš* 'man', *žena* 'woman', *meja* 'border'. Here again the correspondence of content can be stated in terms of translatability and the correspondence of expression in terms of phoneme correspondences as to the place in respective strings: *r:r, ǫ:o, k:k, a:a, m:m, ž:š, ь:Ø, ž:ž, e:e, n:n, đ:j*.

Since the relation of correspondence is symmetric and transitive, the application of the operators on Proto-Slavic words did not establish correspondences only between them and the Serbo-Croatian or Slovene words respectively but also between the latter two languages. The correspondence of content can again best be stated by translatability which in this case can be checked empirically. The correspondence of expression amounts again to a set of phoneme correspondences: *r*:*r*, *u*:*o*, *k*:*k*, *a*:*a*, *m*:*m*, *ž*:*š*, *Ø*:*Ø*, *ž*:*ž*, *e*:*e*, *n*:*n*, *d*:*j*.

So regular sound change can always be traced by its effects consisting in phonemic correspondences of a certain kind. It will therefore be necessary to investigate in some detail the notion of correspondence as used in comparative linguistics.

Internal language change is not confined to sound change. On higher levels too, some regularity in the relation between the replacing language and the replaced one should be expected. Here again it must be possible to express the process of internal change as a transformation the operator of which is statable in terms of linguistic units of the respective rank. Thus the operator of morphological change can be stated in terms of morphologic entities. Operator rules, that are most general and uniform, can be stated in terms of allomorphs. Thus the substitution of all English -*en* plurals except that of *ox* by -*s* plurals can in a general form be stated only for the -*en* allomorph of the plural morpheme as defined by its morphemic surroundings, one of which, namely *ox*, prevents the substitution by -*s*. These morphologic rules are much more complex and less integrated than sound laws are. That is not so because the change process in morphology is less regular, but because the morphological system in itself is less simple and integrated.

In an analogous way, syntactic change can be expressed by transformations with operator rules that can be stated in terms of syntactic markers as defined by certain surroundings. Thus Greek ὑπό in surroundings defining it as the marker of the expression of the agent in passive clauses has been substituted by ἀπό in Modern Greek, while in other surroundings it has been replaced otherwise. It is the same regularity principle that underlies replacements in internal change on all levels of linguistic structure.

Morphological and syntactic change establish correspondences analogous to the phonemic ones.

5

CORRESPONDENCE IN COMPARATIVE LINGUISTICS

The effects of regular sound change are phonemic correspondences between forms of two or more languages and they are most important evidence for genetic relationship. Correspondence is therefore a fundamental notion of comparative linguistics.

We have seen already that the concept of correspondence is indispensable to the taxonomic theory of language in order to account for the restrictions of linguistic diversity (cf. chapter 2). There are also different types of correspondences. One of them is characteristic for genetic relationship. It is the type of correspondence which appears as the effect of regular sound change. Regular sound change is in its turn correlated with internal language change and the letter defines genetic relationship. Thus genetic relationship can be established with the help of phonemic correspondences.

The phonemic correspondences in correspondent forms of two or more languages form strings which can in their turn be analyzed on a higher level. It is on this basis that a comparative morphology is possible, but it is not purely morphological because it presupposes comparative phonology. Morphological correspondences which do not include phonemic ones are by necessity only typological because they cannot be demonstrably connected with internal language change and thus with language descent.

It has been said already that when languages are described in terms of transformational generative models, the concept of correspondence is no longer needed for the description of restricted diversity because such models can have common elements. Restricted diversity is then described by the occurrence of identical rules in the models of the languages.

But in such a presentation of linguistic relationship the correspondence relations are not excluded. They are implicit in the statement of generative processes with identical rules which by necessity generate correspondent units. Therefore genetic relationship can be established only by finding out whether there are characteristic correspondence relations between the languages in question. The correspondences must be dealt with in any case whether in the final description of genetic relationship we shall state them explicitly or not.

As we have seen, phonemic correspondence is the fundamental concept in the systematic description of a genetic relationship. Every group of genetically related languages has its own doctrine of comparative grammar based on the established phonemic correspondences. In the presentation of comparative grammars they are usually assumed to be the basic data accessible to immediate experience and self-evident.

Of all the great systematicians of Indo-European comparative linguistics it was A. Meillet who was most explicit on this subject.[1] The others were less explicit and tend to describe relations implicitly by the statements of sound laws.[2]

In the first place we must investigate the properties of phonemic correspondence which is regarded to be the simplest and most elementary notion of comparative linguistics.[3] It is easy to show that phonemic correspondence as usually introduced in comparative linguistics is not an elementary concept and that it is therefore unacceptable as an undefined and self-evident fundamental notion.

The phonemes of different languages can correspond in many ways. They can correspond in the movements of articulation by which their realization comes about, they can correspond acoustically or as to the restrictions imposed on their distribution in

---

[1] 1937, 41 "... la seule réalité à laquelle elle (comparative linguistics) ait affaire, ce sont les correspondances entre les langues attestées".
[2] Cf. Brugmann (1897, 92ff.) and Hirt (1927, 208ff.).
[3] For this and for what follows cf. Katičić (1966b, 203-220).

phonemic strings. None of these correspondences is relevant to comparative linguistics because they define typological relationship and have no necessary correlation with genetic relationship. Comparative linguistics investigates as its primary data the correspondences of phonemes in regard to their place in phonemic strings. For such is phonemic correspondence resulting from regular sound change.[4]

But, so defined, the phonemic correspondence of comparative linguistics is still not sufficiently determined. For any two phonemic strings have phonemes which correspond as to their place in them. Take for example

Lat.	homoØ	'man'
	| | | | |	
Hebr.	me l ek	'king'.

Such correspondences exist between any pair of phonemic strings. They are a universal and are thus no relevant restriction of diversity. They bear no witness of linguistic relationship and cannot be regarded as the effect of regular sound change.

In order to define properly the phoneme correspondence relevant in comparative linguistics it is necessary to introduce two additional requirements: (1) the phonemic correspondences as to the place in strings must be recurrent and (2) they must occur in strings with correspondent content. These requirements reflect faithfully the properties of internal change and regular sound change as discussed in the preceding chapter.

The first requirement, that of recurrence, introduces a difficult question: how many times must a correspondence of phonemes as to their place in strings recur in order to be accepted as recurrent. If the recurrence requirement remains unspecified, any correspondence occurring more than once fulfills it. But such an unfrequent recurrence may easily be an effect of pure chance because of the limited number of phonemes in all languages. The probability of a chance correspondence is not insignificant enough

---

[4]   Cf. p. 64 ff.

for such correspondences with a small frequency to be accepted as relevant in comparative linguistics. For it is the aim of the recurrence requirement to distinguish those correspondences of phonemes as to their place in strings which are due to historical replacement processes from those which came about by pure chance. Unfrequent recurrences cannot therefore be regarded as satisfactory. But it is also impossible to determine how frequent a recurrence should be in order to be accepted as relevant in comparative linguistics. All that can be done is the statement of a general principle to the effect that the more frequently a phonemic correspondence recurs, the surer it is established in comparative linguistics.

In practice, in the vast majority of cases the difference between a relevant and a non-relevant recurrence is self-evident. Wherever the situation is less favorable there is no obvious solution and things remain unclear. A part of such cases can be brought to a satisfactory solution with the help of the second, the semantic requirement. Where this expedient fails, problems in comparative phonology remain mostly insoluble.

The indispensable and essential requirement of recurrence makes of the correspondence concept as used in comparative phonology a probabilistic notion. It is not given empirically as a discrete unit and on the basis of pure observation we can never say that it does or that it does not exist. In reality we empirically observe only a continuous statistical distribution which must be quantified in the most convenient way into relevant and irrelevant recurrences in order to get the phonemic correspondences needed for the establishment of genetic relationship. This quantification is an essential part of the comparative method but in the usual presentation it is not explicit. There only the results are stated without an account of how they model the immediately given reality and of the alternative choices that were presented by this reality.

Many difficult problems in Indo-European phonology do not allow a satisfactory solution because the best quantification of the statistical data is not self-evident and it cannot be decided whether the recurrence requirement is satisfied or not. An example of such a problem are the Indo-European voiceless aspirates or the Greek correspondence of, for example, ə. The correspondence of Skr. *aham* 'I', *mahat* 'big', *duhitr̥* 'daughter' with Gr. ἐγώ 'I', μέγας 'big', θυγάτηρ 'daughter' belongs to the same category.

Any attempt to solve these much debated questions ignoring the fundamental problems of methodology and searching only for arguments and indications supporting a favoured solution remains by necessity on the surface. It will contribute to the variety of opinions instead of helping to understand its roots.

The difference between the traditional and the laryngealist correspondences is of the same nature. The heated discussion that arose about the laryngeal theory could become much more fruitful if the methodological problems were made explicit. It would then appear that the theoretical foundations of comparative linguistics are involved in this dispute. The notion of phonemic correspondence, insufficiently precise as it is now, allows such different presentations of quite the same linguistic data. A theoretical approach to this question would surely help to improve comparative linguistics as a method even if it could not solve the problem of whether and how many laryngeals there were in Proto-Indo-European. We could say at least why no answer can be found.

The second essential requirement of correspondence of content is very far-reaching in its implications. Because of it, phonemic correspondence, which is usually regarded as a simple and self-evident concept in comparative linguistics, in reality presupposes the correspondence of content. And content has until now been least of all investigated in linguistics. Even after the recent progress made in semantic theory we are still unable to formulate in a satisfactory way the requirement of correspondent content.[5] Phonemic correspondence thus, cannot for the time being, be defined with all the necessary precision.

It could seem that correspondence of content is not really necessary for the definition of phonemic correspondence. If this was

---

[5]   Cf. Kronasser (1952) and especially Hjelmslev (1953). For the most recent and very important work cf. Katz-Fodor (1963), Katz-Postal (1964) and Chomsky (1965).

true, much trouble could be avoided. Phonemic correspondence would in such a case be determined simply as a recurrent correspondence of phonemes as to their place in strings. Their recurrence would be sufficient to distinguish them from random correspondences which are the product of pure chance.

Unfortunately, it is easy to show, that such a definition of phonemic correspondence is untenable. For the phonemic correspondences can be established by recurrence alone only if the interpretation of the statistical distribution is self-evident and regular recurrence distinctly different from random repetitions. But there are cases of genetically relevant correspondences which have no evidently relevant recurrence. Thus Skr. *aham* and Gr. ἐγώ can be regarded as an instance of the correspondence γ:h only because both have the content 'I'. The correspondence ε:a would in itself not be enough to establish that the forms are phonemically correspondent, and the correspondence γ:h is not recurrent enough in order to be recognized on that evidence alone as a phonemic correspondence in the sense of comparative linguistics. The correspondence of whole strings is thus again a matter of probability. The more correspondences they contain which are not likely due to chance the more probable it becomes that the strings are themselves correspondent.

But even there, where the identification of correspondences can be managed with recurrence alone, it may be impossible to identify an individual case of correspondence without the criterion of content. Thus for Slovenian and Serbo-Croatian the following phonemic correspondences can be established beyond any doubt on the evidence of recurrence alone: o:o, o:u, p:p, t:t. Slovenian *pot* 'way' can hence correspond to Serbo-Croatian *pot* 'sweat' and to Serbo-Croatian *put* 'way'. Only the content can show that in this instance the second equation is the correct one and we have an instance of the correspondence o:u and not of o:o. Hence it is necessary to define phonemic correspondence in comparative linguistics as a recurrent correspondence of phonemes as to their position in strings which serve to express corresponding contents.

Things being as they are we are forced to define content correspondence as well as we can. To a certain degree this must be possible since comparative linguistics has already successfully worked with it for many decades. These rich experiences make it possible to state a workable definition which under the present conditions must remain unsatisfactory from a theoretical point of view and therefore also only of limited practical value. Translatability is the criterion used most frequently in comparative research. It can be stated in a narrower and in a broader sense. In the first case it will be asked whether the forms in question usually translate each other. In the second all pairs of forms will be included which can translate each other, however rare or far-fetched they may be.

Such a wider definition of content correspondence has definite advantages for it takes even semantic change to a certain extent into consideration. Words that translate each other most commonly tend in semantic change to develop such contents which can be substituted for each other in translation only in certain contexts or metaphorically and with a special stylistic value.[6] But there are semantic changes which do not leave even such broadly defined translatability. Because of well-established phonemic correspondences there is no doubt that Skr. *dhūmas* 'smoke' and OChSl. *dymъ* 'smoke' are cognates of Gr. θῡμός 'soul, anger', and hence the content of these words should be accepted as correspondent. And yet it is in any case impossible to translate Homers οὐχ οἱ ἥνδανε θυμῷ by 'it did not please him in his smoke'. One can well see, of course, how this difference in content came about by metaphoric semantic change. But it is very difficult to formulate criteria which will help to distinguish the result of metaphorical semantic change from the possibility to use the content of a morpheme metaphorically. For it is not enough to show that a certain metaphoric usage is possible in order to prove that it actually became the starting point of a semantic change.

Phonemic correspondence, as used in comparative linguistics, presupposes thus the correspondence of content. But it must

---

[6]   Cf. Hoenigswald (1960, 27ff.).

reckon with semantic change or else it will fail to establish the real genetic relationships between the phonemic strings of two or more languages. If the concept phonemic correspondence is to provide for the differentiation of the content of genetically related phonemic strings, the correspondence of content it presupposes cannot be maximal. Thus Goth. *saihvan* corresponds phonemically to Lat. *sequor* and hence they correspond also as to their content. But Goth. *saihvan* and Lat. *aspicere* correspond better in this respect.[7]

The correspondence of content is no discrete unit and hence it admits graduality. It is very important to make the concept of content correspondence more precise so that it can be better used for the purposes of comparative linguistics. Only so it may become possible to discover underlying regularities in semantic change and to arrive by means of it to a quantification of the correspondences of content which present themselves, for the time being, as a continuum. Every progress in semantic theory can help us to arrive at this aim. It is certainly not enough to search for parallel cases in support of a supposed semantic change. And it is precisely in this latter way that one has tried to solve the doubtful cases.

In practice recurrence and correspondence of content complement each other and help thus very much to establish the phonemic correspondences. Just as the correspondence of content can help to decide whether two strings of phonemes are correspondent or not, the content of two phonemic strings with well established recurrent phonemic correspondences is likely to be also corre-

---

[7] This requirement of content correspondence which is not necessarily maximal is a consequence of the fact that genetic relationship of languages manifests itself as a simultaneous typological relationship of the content and the expression. Cf. Greenberg (1957) and Uspenskij (1965, 31). In such an approach even minor typological correspondence may become relevant if it is the only one connected with typological correspondence of its expression and vice versa. Thus Engl. *mother* and Albanian *motër* 'sister' do not correspond typologically either in expression or in content, for Albanian has a voiced dental fricative in its phonemic system and the word *mëmë* 'mother' in its vocabulary while English has a voiceless dental stop and the word *sister*. But if both expression and content are taken into account, there is no Albanian word which corresponds more typologically to Engl. *mother* than Alb. *motër*.

spondent. This complementing of the recurrence of phonemic correspondences as to their place in strings by the correspondence of their contents and vice versa is precisely the way by which comparative linguistics has come to its remarkable successes. But there are numerous cases where it did not yield satisfactory results because the conditions are less favourable in other languages and language groups and the genetic relationships less evident. These cases show how necessary it is to inquire into the theoretical foundations of comparative linguistics and to examine its fundamental assumptions, only so this method can become adequate to its yet unsolved tasks.

The results of this short inquiry show that phonemic correspondence in comparative linguistics is (1) a correspondence of phonemes as to their position in strings, (2) that this correspondence is recurrent, the more frequently it recurs the more probable it is that the correspondence has been set up correctly and (3) that the phonemic strings express morphemes with correspondent contents, the surer this correspondence the greater the significance of an observed recurrence of correspondence of phonemes as to their place in strings for the setting up of phonemic correspondences.

The above propositions, though undoubtedly important for the understanding of the theoretical nature of phonemic correspondence, as set up in comparative linguistics, do not describe it fully. For in the systematic presentations of Indo-European comparative linguistics only a part of all the correspondences that satisfy the conditions stated above is given the status of phonemic correspondences. For instance, in the systematic presentations only

(a) Skr. *t*   Lat. *t*   Germ. *þ*

is given such a status while

(b) Skr. *t*   Lat. *t*   Germ. *d*

is treated as a special case of the same phonemic correspondence although it satisfies for itself all the conditions for a phonemic correspondence according to the criteria mentioned above. The same can be said of

(c)   Skr. *t*   Lat. *t*   Germ. *t*.

Both (b) and (c) are denied the full status of phonemic correspondences in the current systematic presentations. The reason for it is easily seen. In all languages except Germanic these correspondences are represented by the same phonemes. They differ only in Germanic and even there they are in complementary distribution so that it is always possible to predict by the phonemic surroundings which of them will appear in any given case. It is hence sufficient for an accurate description of these relations to state the differences only for Germanic with an indication of the conditions for their appearance. That amounts to a full description of their distribution.

It can thus be shown that what we currently know as phonemic correspondences from the textbooks of Indo-European linguistics are not all the recurrent correspondences of phonemes occurring in morphs which belong to morphemes with correspondent content, but only a carefully selected subset of them to which the whole rest can be reduced by appropriate rules for each language. The idea, suggested by some textbooks (especially Meillets) that the phonemic correspondences set up in their presentation of the doctrine are the fundamental empirical data of comparative linguistics must be discarded. In reality they are a highly complex and sophisticated system in which the results arrived at by comparative research are presented.

As in every system of presentation, in setting up phonemic correspondences one has to choose among alternative possibilities. If the immediately given reality is to be the starting point of the presentation, it is necessary to establish first all the recurrent correspondences of phonemes as to their place in morphs which belong to morphemes with correspondent content accounting thereby explicitly for all quantifications that underlie the established correspondences. After this is done the correspondences will afterwards be treated as units, and new symbols will be introduced, one for each of them. The fundamental correspondences can be conveniently formalized if we fix the order by which the phonemes representing the correspondences in the compared languages are stated. Every correspondence becomes then a unit composed by other units arranged in a fixed order. In mathematics such units are called vectors and it is most convenient to think of phonemic correspondences as vectors.

The established correspondences become then in their turn the subject of a new classification. The aim of that classification is to gather in classes such correspondences which have a complementary distribution in phonemic strings and which differ as little as possible as to the phonemes by which they are made up. Such classes become then in their turn units of a higher rank. Our correspondences (a), (b), (c) form such a class. It will be represented by that of its members which has the least restricted distribution. In our example this will be (a).

Such classes of vectors we shall provisionally call independent correspondences. In practice these independent correspondences will very often be classes with one member. The correspondences stated in the systematic presentations are in fact correspondences representative of independent correspondences. Hoenigswald has described and illustrated the procedure of classifying phonemic correspondences into independent correspondences.[8] In principle it is identical with the classification of allophones into phonemes as practiced in classical phonemics. The phonological correspondences can hence be equated to allophones and the independent correspondences with phonemes. The whole procedure is in fact an attempt to establish the phonemic system of the proto-language as coded in the phonemic correspondences of genetically related languages.

Because the sound laws which determine the substitution of phonological entities in sound change can be formulated without further specifications only for the allophones of the older language, these allophones will be coded in the phonemic correspondences. Only by classifying them into independent correspondences one can hope to arrive at the phonemic system of the common older stage of genetically related languages.

[8]   Cf. (1950), (1960, 132) and Hockett (1965, 188).

But the procedure of classification is identical only in principle. While in the case of allophones their distribution is given directly by the recorded texts, the original distribution of phonemic correspondences must be reconstructed first. In comparative linguistics, the effects of analogical change are to be reckoned with. Analogy is the basic mechanism of morphic redistribution, *i.e.*, of morphological change. Analogical sound change is nothing but the phonemic implications of morphological change. By it, the original distribution of phonemes in the languages compared will always be altered to a greater or lesser extent. The complementary distribution of phonemic correspondences can only very seldom be read directly from the recorded texts but it must be inferred from the attested distribution. This means that in practice only a part of the distribution must be selected as relevant and the rest disregarded. Only so the original complementary distribution can be restored. Criteria for such a selection can be obtained only by careful consideration of the question which positions are more exposed to analogical change than others. It is, for instance, quite clear that phonemes in positions where they are members of a morphoneme may easily be replaced analogically by another member of the morphoneme which has a wider distribution in the morphological system. In selecting relevant distributions such positions will then be disregarded.

The replacement of Indo-European labiovelars in Greek is here a case in question. The original distribution: a dental before *i* and *e* and a labial in other positions cannot be read from the recorded material. It must be inferred from the real distribution of phonemic correspondences. Many instances in which labials are found before *i* and *e* such as λείπετε 'you leave' are in positions where labial and velar originally belonged to one morphoneme: cf. λείπομεν 'we leave' *λείτετε 'you leave', λείπουσι 'they leave'. It is very probable that in such a position one allomorph has been replaced by the other, especially if the latter is more frequent. In other positions, where the morphophonemic relation is less conspicuous the supposed original distribution occurs more often than not as for instance in τίσις 'recompense' and ποινή 'blood money', or τίς 'who' and πότερος 'which one of two'. It is clear that these cases weigh heavier for the selection of the original distribution than the others do, and they allow thus to infer from the just described situation what the sound laws were which transformed the Indo-European labio-velars into Greek labials and dentals and determined thus their original distribution.

The distribution of correspondences relevant to comparative linguistics is not that one that can be read from the attested forms but only a selection from it which we can only more or less convincingly prove to be the most probable original distribution. Just as phonemic correspondence itself, its distribution is in last analysis also a probabilistic concept.

The system of presentation of the results of comparative research that was sketched above conforms well with the methodological requirements of taxonomic linguistic theory. In it the structural principles are made explicit which underlie the whole edifice of doctrine built up by the traditional comparativists. But such a description of the correspondence relations is much too cumbersome to be really useful. Even if it is expressed in the most economic way, it remains indispensable to state at least once all phonemic correspondences in every independent correspondence. That means that the same relations of correspondence will be stated more than once. Even in our extremely simple example of the independent correspondence {(a), (b), (c)}, it will be indispensable to state three times the correspondence $t:t$ for Sanskrit and Latin: once in stating (a), once in stating (b) and once more in stating (c). This redundancy can be avoided if, instead of stating the correspondences and classifying them into independent correspondences, we introduce a set of ordered rules which apply to a chosen set of initial symbols and generate all the correspondence relations that are to be described.

Such a generative description of sound correspondences is easily done. It is necessary to select in every independent correspondence a phonemic correspondence to serve as a starting point, whereas the others will be treated as its modifications. Usually it may be that one which represents the whole independent correspondence. In our example it may hence be (a). If the replacement rules in the description are expressed by logical implications, the whole may assume this form:

> T is given
> (1) → T $\langle t \; t \; þ \rangle$
> (2) → þ (after s, h, f) t
> (3) → þ (when not after stressed vowel) d.

The ordered set $\langle t \; t \; þ \rangle$ is a vector composed of an Old-Indian, a Latin and a Germanic phoneme in that succession fixed for the whole description. It is this vector that states the basic correspondence relation generated by the rules, whereas the other rules specify its modifications.

It is by no means sure and must be specially investigated whether the choice of (a) was optimal when judged by the economy of the whole system of presentation of phonemic correspondences between Old-Indian, Latin and Germanic. Perhaps it could be shown that rule (1) should preferably be replaced by

> (4) → T $\langle t \; t \; t \rangle$

and rule (3) by

> (5) → germ. t (when not after s, f, h) þ.

The rule (3) could remain as it is. From the point of view of this description the first alternative is clearly preferable because it differentiates the germanic phoneme already in the vector and so it is not necessary to specify in the following rule that it applies only to the germanic member of the vector.

It is easy to see that all phonemic correspondences can be described in this way without unnecessary repetitions. Such a generative description is therefore clearly preferable to the other one which states only items and their arrangement and it is often applied in textbooks when they describe correspondence relations by saying that x in proto-X became y in Y and z in Z.

The replacements formulated in the rules (1), (2), (3) are quite abstract operations in the frame of a generative description. But they can also receive a historical interpretation as sound change that actually happened. In the current systematic presentations of phonemic correspondences, the replacements operated by generative rules are not distinguished from historical events. And when this distinction is neglected, historical statements can be used for the description of correspondence relations. In this sense it is true that history helps to explain existing relations.

Nevertheless it is necessary to distinguish strictly a dynamic description by operations from their historical interpretation. As our example has shown, there can be more equivalent dynamic descriptions of the same correspondence relations. All such descriptions are correct. But if they were interpreted historically, only one such interpretation can be correct. Hence there is no justification to identify both concepts as traditional comparative linguistics tends to do.

For progress in this field, it is essential to find some criteria in order to select from all possible equivalent generative descriptions the one that can with most probability be interpreted historically. Even if it should prove impossible to find really satisfactory criteria for that purpose, the search for them will by itself help to improve our understanding of the theoretical foundations of comparative linguistics. The well-known traditional study of languages is always simultaneously a generative description of languages and language families. It is for this reason that many linguists contend that language history helps to understand language. Only emotional involvement or doctrinary narrow-mindedness can induce a linguist to deny the descriptive function and explanatory power of historical grammar.[9]

The concept of morphological correspondence in comparative linguistics must by the nature of things be even more complex than that of phonemic correspondence. And yet it is of fundamental importance for the clearing of questions that arise in the genetic classification of languages for which it furnishes the essen-

[9] On language history as the most adequate description in some cases cf. Halle (1962, 342ff.), Klima (1964), Saporta (1965).

tial criterion. The next pages will therefore be devoted to an inquiry into its properties.

In comparative morphology a morphological correspondence does not designate any correspondence of morphological systems but only a very definite kind of them, namely those for which there is reason to believe that they are an effect of internal change. The way in which the systematic presentations and textbooks of comparative linguistics introduce morphology is not always apt to give a correct idea of the nature of morphological correspondence. In Indo-European linguistics, it is usually the typological correspondence of the older stages of the Indo-European languages which is described and stressed and the correspondence of grammatical categories is being established on the basis of broader-defined translatability. The system of typological correspondences, so established, is then regarded as the system of categories of the proto-language. Afterwards the phonemic correspondences in the expression of those categories in all the related languages are stated.

Although this procedure leads in the case of Indo-European to results of evidently high relevance, it cannot be accepted without objection because it treats typological correspondence as if it were an essential criterion for morphological correspondence in comparative linguistics. And yet, typological correspondences can be found even among such languages for which there is no reason whatsoever to assume a genetic relationship while the typological relationship of unquestionably cognate languages may be much less close. There is, of course, a very definite correlation between genetic and typological relationship, especially in morphology. It is always very probable that genetically related languages will show also a certain degree of typological relationship. But the contrary is not true since typological relationship may, as far as we know, very well occur without genetic relationship. Morphological correspondence can therefore in comparative linguistics not be defined as the typological correspondence of grammatical content and of the rules by which lexical and grammatical morphemes are combined into words.

The morphological correspondences in comparative linguistics must be the effect of regular sound change for this is the only way to prove internal change by linguistic data. Morphological correspondence must hence be defined by phonemic correspondence. Typological correspondences are of course a welcome additional indication, especially valuable for any attempt at a reconstruction of the morphological system of the proto-language, but in the definition of morphological correspondence it is better left out since it does not determine genetic relationship but is only to a certain extent determined by it.

The concept of morphological correspondence thus presupposes phonemic correspondence. It can perhaps best be defined as phonemic correspondence of parts of phonemic strings which serve as the expression of words. Such strings we shall call word-forms. Morphological correspondence is the phonemic correspondence of any parts of two word-forms belonging to two different languages but only of such parts which have the same position with respect to the other parts of the word forms compared. Consequently, in the word-forms of the languages under comparison such parts correspond morphologically which (1) correspond phonemically and (2) have the same position in respect to one or more parts of the word forms concerned: both must be on the right end of the word-forms or both on the left end or both in the middle. The word-forms to which such parts belong can also be said to correspond morphologically.

The most striking property of this definition is that it denies relevance for morphological correspondence almost to the whole morphological structure of the languages compared. At first glance this may seem confusing. The only morphological concept in the definition is that of the word which as a linguistic unit determines the upper boundary of morphology. The word consists of morphemes arranged in a fixed order. Since morphology describes the rules by which morphemes are selected into words, the fixed order of morphemes in the word is a morphological universal.

Only this most general and universal property of morphological systems can be taken for granted in the definition of morphological correspondences because all other properties of morphological structure may be altered in language change. In defining morphological correspondence it cannot be taken for granted that any one of these even remotely possible changes did not happen. All details of the morphological structure of genetically related languages can be very much different. Therefore it is not the morphemic structure of words which we expect to be necessarily correspondent in genetically related languages but only the fixed order of morphologically unspecified parts of word-forms. The morphological status of these parts may be different in different related languages.

It is likely that everybody will agree that Skr. *agnes* and Goth. *qênais* realize a morphological correspondence. This is in full accordance with our definition as given above, for the right parts of both word-forms *-es* and *-ais* are phonemically correspondent. Thus both conditions for morphological correspondence of two word-forms are fulfilled. But if a correspondent morphological status was required for the phonemically correspondent parts, it would be difficult to establish the correspondence because the morphemic boundary is different in Old Indic and Gothic:

$$agne|s \qquad qên|ais.$$

According to the definition given above, *agnes* is morphologically correspondent also with Lat. *ignis* or *ignem*, for in these word-forms the left parts *agn-* and *ign-* are correspondent phonemically. Here too the morphological status of the phonemically correspondent parts is different. The morphemic boundary is *agne|s* and *ign|is* respectively. This case can be distinguished from the first mentioned one by the fact that in one the phonemically correspondent parts include the morphs of grammatical morphemes while in the other they include the morphs of lexical morphemes. Such additional criteria make it possible to account for this very important difference while the fundamental equivalence of both cases remains expressed by the fact that both must be fully recognized as morphological correspondences.

A complete phonemic correspondence of word-forms is but a

special case of morphological correspondence. Cf. Skr. *agnis*, Lat. *ignis*, OChSl. *ognъ*. Morphological correspondence can be established by any part of these word forms. It can also be said that, as a whole, they are phonemically correspondent and that they have the same position towards the zero word-form parts at their right or at their left or both: Ø *agnis* Ø, Ø *ignis* Ø, Ø *ognъ* Ø.

Such complete phonemic correspondences of word forms are exceptionally favorable for comparative morphology. Synchronic morphological analysis can there be applied to strings of phonemic correspondences representing word forms of the proto-language. But the establishing of morphological correspondences cannot be confined to such most favorable cases for morphological change does not consist only in a morphemic reorganization of word-forms subject to sound change but also in a change of the rules by which morphemes are composed into words and morphs into word-forms.

In Ital. *capire*, *capisco* all morphs are transforms of latin morphs to which the operator of spontaneous regular sound change is applied. New and non-Latin is only the possibility to compose them into word forms that are grammatical. In Latin *-ī-re* and *-isc-* cannot be combined with *cap-* although all these morphs exist in the language. Therefore a general theory of comparative linguistics must foresee the possibility that all original combinations of morphs have been altered. The Latin conjugation in *-isco* could be established by the comparison of Romance languages even if the lexical morphemes belonging to the Romance word-forms of this conjugation had no single phonemically correspondent morph. Even then it would be possible to know that in Proto-Romance there existed a conjugation in *-isco* although no verb belonging to it could be named with any certainty. By not requiring complete phonemic correspondence of word-forms for the establishment of morphological correspondences such possibilities are provided for. Morphological analysis can be performed on the attested strings of phonemic correspondences.

In comparative morphology, what is really compared, are usu-ally not single word-forms but whole paradigms or at least fragments of paradigms.[10] Those paradigms of two languages which have most morphologically corresponding word-forms constitute what we shall call a morphologically corresponding pair of paradigms. The paradigms of Skr. *devas* 'god' and Goth. *dags* 'day' constitute, for instance, such a pair because there is no paradigm in Gothic which has more word-forms which correspond morphologically with those of the paradigm of Skr. *devas*. Of course, since the relation of correspondence is a symmetric relation, the reverse is also true.

As has been stressed at the beginning of this discussion of morphological correspondence in comparative linguistics, the correspondence of content in itself cannot be accepted as directly relevant for the establishment of morphological correspondences. Since morphological correspondence presupposes phonemic correspondence and the latter is defined by correspondence of content among other fundamental concepts, this latter correspondence is indirectly relevant for morphological correspondence also. But, as has been shown in an earlier part of this chapter (cf. p. 74) this content correspondence is not necessarily the most close one. Maximal correspondences of content are relevant rather to typological than to genetic research. But in combination with morphological correspondence, maximal correspondence of content can be most useful in comparative morphology. The only important thing is not to overlook the fundamental difference between the two concepts while using them simultaneously. In fact, the most remarkable results in Indo-European comparative morphology have been achieved by a combined application of both.

In order to account for this state of things it will be necessary to introduce a new type of correspondence combining both morphological correspondence and typological correspondence of content. This new type we shall call paradigmatical correspondence. Two word forms of two different languages correspond paradigmatically if each of them belongs to a paradigm which constitutes with the other a correspondent pair and if the content of the two

---

[10]   For the concept of paradigm in morphology cf. Seiler (1967).

word-forms corresponds more than that of any two other word-forms belonging each to one of the paradigms which constitute the corresponding pair. It is irrelevant for paradigmatical correspondence whether the word-forms in question are themselves morphologically correspondent or not. This means that not a single part of theirs must be phonemically correspondent. The paradigms to which they belong ought to constitute a correspondent pair but this relation can be determined by other members and not by those which are under scrutiny for paradigmatic correspondence. The forms Skr. *agnes* (gen. sg.) and Goth. *qênais* (gen. sg.) are correspondent both morphologically and paradigmatically. But this combination is by no means a logical necessity. The forms Lat. *cervorum* (gen. pl.) and Goth. *dagê* (gen. pl.) are correspondent paradigmatically but not morphologically. Only their paradigms constitute a morphologically correspondent pair. On the other side, OChSl. *ženy* (nom. pl.) and Lat. *terras* (acc. pl.) correspond morphologically, since *-y* and *-as* correspond phonemically, but they do not correspond paradigmatically since their content is not more correspondent than that of any other two forms belonging each to one of the two paradigms.

Morphological correspondence presupposes, as has been said, correspondence of content but not maximal. In paradigmatic correspondence it is only maximal content correspondence which is relevant. Therefore the two are concepts to a certain extent independent of each other. This independence is not total in so far as paradigmatic correspondence presupposes correspondent pairs of paradigms and these presuppose in their turn morphologic correspondence. But not all members of a correspondent pair of paradigms ought to be morphologically correspondent. A pair of word-forms may therefore be paradigmatically correspondent while not corresponding morphologically.

With the concepts of correspondence hitherto introduced it becomes possible to describe very accurately the method of comparative morphology and to make explicit the criteria for the fundamental decisions that must be made in such work. In Indo-European comparative morphology there is a general consensus that a paradigm or rather the fragment of a paradigm should be reconstructed as containing the forms: *so ek'wos - toi ek'wōs*. The reason for this general consensus can now explicitly be stated as follows: in paradigmatically correspondent word-forms a part of the Indo-European languages has a morphologic correspondence defined by the phonemic correspondence *-ōs* and another part of them a morphological correspondence defined by *-oi*. In such cases it is indicated to suppose that an original complementary distribution of morphs has been destroyed by analogical change. Such a complementary distribution still exists in Indo-Iranian and Germanic. On this basis, it is indicated to assume the same complementary distribution for the proto-language which is supposed to have distinguished a nominal paradigm with a nom.pl. in *-ōs* and a pronominal one with a nom.pl.m. in *-oi*. The whole state of things can be presented in this form:

| Indo-European languages | nom.pl.m. | |
	nominal o-stems	pronominal stems
Indo-Iranian	*-ōs*	*-oi*
Germanic	*-ōs*	*-oi*
Greek	*-oi*	*-oi*
Latin	*-oi*	*-oi*
Osco-Umbrian	*-ōs*	*-ōs*
Baltic	*-oi*	*-oi*
Slavic	*-oi*	*-oi*

The supposed complementary distribution of the morphs in the proto-language can be expressed by two morphological correspondences with complementary distribution:

$$\boxed{\text{pronominal stem}} \quad \textit{-oi}$$

and

$$\boxed{\text{nominal stem}} \quad \textit{-ōs}$$

as the expression of "nom.pl.(m.)" in the Indo-European proto-language.

In such a way every argumentation in comparative morphology can be made easy to survey and it is clear that in such a succinct presentation the merits and shortcomings of every opinion will become more conspicuous.

Such a search for the underlying regularities in the morphological correspondence relations among languages is very much akin to the morphological description of a language. In fact, it is a search for the morphological system of the proto-language which is coded into the correspondence relations among the morphological systems of genetically related languages. But here again, the original distributions cannot be directly read from the corpus as it is the case, at least in principle, in descriptive linguistics. Analogical change has often profoundly altered the distribution of corresponding morphs. It is therefore necessary to infer the original distribution from the recorded ones and this is even more difficult than in comparative phonology. In principle, it is done in the same way, namely by trying to decide which of the recorded distributions is most informative. In our example case the repetition of the grammatical morphs is redundant in all languages except Indo-Iranian and Germanic. It is precisely this informativity which makes so plausible the assumption that the Indo-Iranian and the Germanic distribution is the original one.

We can say but little about syntactic correspondences in comparative linguistics. On this field much less has been done until now than in comparative phonology and morphology. There is no rich experience from which we could abstract the fundamental notions of comparative syntax. Delbrück's remarkable work remained more or less a parallel syntax of the archaic Indo-European languages and it concentrates basically on their typological comparison. And yet it is essential for comparative syntax as for any other field of comparative linguistics to distinguish genetic from typological correspondence.

In recent time very interesting and stimulating results have been achieved in comparative syntax especially on the basis of Anatolian data.[11] And this substantial progress shows clearly that in syntax

[11]   Cf. Ivanov (1965, 185f.).

also a purely genetic approach is possible and that it can be fruitful. There is, of course, a definite correlation between genetic and typological relationship in syntax as elsewhere. But here again genetic correspondence implies a certain typological correspondence but not necessarily a maximal one. It is very interesting that substantial progress has been achieved in comparative Indo-European syntax only after such languages with a typologically aberrant syntax as Hittite and Irish were compared.[12]

Since regular sound change is the only linguistic effect of internal change that can positively be identified, the concept of syntactic correspondence must presuppose phonemic correspondence. But it is also clear that a full phonemic correspondence of the syntagms and sentences compared cannot be required. Such fully correspondent syntagms as Skr. *śravas akšitam* and Gr. κλέος ἄφθιτον both 'unfading glory' can be found but they are rare and we learn little from them about the syntax, especially the sentence, of the proto-language. Comparative syntax cannot confine itself to that kind of data, though, when available, they are of the utmost value. It is necessary to insist on the phonemic and morphological correspondence of only such morphs which serve as the expression of morphemes essential for the syntactic pattern of sentences and classes, *i.e.*, of syntactic markers.

As in morphology, it will in syntax also be impossible to include the morphological status of corresponding phonemic strings into the definition of correspondence. Morphological status is not stable enough for that. So we may say that syntactic correspondence in comparative linguistics is a correspondence of sentences, clauses or syntagms with phonemically correspondent strings serving as the expression of at least a part of those morphemes which mark the syntactic relations. These morphemes cannot be specified more closely because they may be grammatical morphemes integrated with lexical morphemes into words and they may also be conjunctions and pronouns which mark sentence structure. According to this definition the sentences: Hit. *nu-mu* ᵈIŠTAR *kanniśan harta* 'and Ishtar loved me' and OIr. *no-m*

---

[12]   Cf. Ivanov (1965, 185ff.).

Choimmdiu-coíma 'the Lord loves me' are syntactically correspondent because the particle *nu* in Hittite and *no* in Old Irish are phonemically correspondent and have both the same syntactic function to mark the introduction of a new sentence. To this initial particle the enclitical object form of the pronoun is added and it too is phonemically and morphologically correspondent in both languages. This whole initial complex defines the syntactical correspondence of the two sentences.

Another pair of syntactically correspondent sentences are Hit. *takkuš* LÚ - *iš wemiyazi tuš* (= *ta + uš*) *kuenzi* 'if the husband finds them, he kills them' (*i.e.*, he may kill them) and OChSl. *ašte li hošteši ... to sъhrani zapovědi* 'if you want ..., keep the commandments' because *ta* in Hittite and *to* in Old-Church-Slavonic are phonemically and morphologically correspondent and they have the same syntactical function of introducing a main clause after a subordinate one.

A further example is Skr. *aśvo ratham vahati* 'the horse draws the charriot', Gr. ἄνϑρωπος ἀσκὸν πίμπλησι 'the man fills the wineskin' and Lat. *alumnus magistrum venerat* 'the disciple venerates the master'. The syntactic correspondence can be established by the fact that the relation of subject, predicate and direct object is in the three languages marked by phonemically and morphologically correspondent morphemes: *-os*, *-om*, *-ti*. If we compare with the above cited Sanskrit sentence Lat. *equus currum vehit* 'the horse draws the charriot', the syntactic correspondence goes even further since the phonemically and morphologically correspondent units are now: *ek'wos*, *-om*, *weg'heti*.

Thus conceived, syntactic correspondence provides a means to investigate genetic relationship in syntax, a task that has been rather neglected till now. The typological correspondence in syntax does by itself bear no witness of genetic affiliation. Here again it is only the traces of regular sound change which provide us with the data necessary for the establishment of genetic relationship. It is because of this that syntactic correspondence presupposes morphological and hence by necessity phonemic correspondence. The easily observed syntactical relationship of Indo-European

languages can on that basis be proved to be genetic. Even the
somehow peculiar Hittite syntax, which is typologically more different than the syntaxes of most ancient Indo-European languages
are among themselves, can by its syntactic correspondences be
shown to be closely genetically related to all of them.[13]

In cases like Skr. *śravas akšitam* and Gr. κλέος ἄφθιτον 'unfading glory' where whole syntagms or even whole sentences are
morphologically and phonemically correspondent we have full
syntactic correspondence. Such full correspondence can be regarded as a special case of syntactic correspondence just as full
morphological correspondence is a special case of morphological
correspondence. The whole syntagm is here the unit that corresponds morphologically and phonemically.

There is a fundamental similarity between morphological and
syntactic correspondence. This is only to be expected because
the traditional boundary between morphology and syntax is not
a very clear one and there are linguists who deny its existence or
at least its importance. In both cases, we have to do with phonemic
correspondence of syntactic markers. In comparative morphology
their integration into words is relevant, whereas in syntax it is
their syntactical function which counts regardless of their status
in respect to words. Here, as in descriptive linguistics, it is the
word boundary that marks the very uncertain border line between
morphology and syntax. Morphological correspondence of word
forms can be defined by the phonemic correspondence of grammatical and lexical morphs, whereas in syntactic correspondence
only the syntactic markers are relevant. This lack of symmetry
accounts for the fact that the correspondence of Gr. νύξ and
OChSl. *noštь*, both 'night' must be accepted as a fact of morphology while there is definitely no syntactic correspondence between
Skr. *pitā sūnuṃ paśyati* 'the father looks at the son' and Gr. ἐν
ὀνόματι τοῦ πατρὸς καὶ τοῦ υἱοῦ 'in the name of the father and
the son', although these two sentences contain some morphologically correspondent word-forms (*pitā* and πατρός, *sūnum* and
υἱοῦ).

[13]   Cf. Ivanov (1965, 186f.).

The word being defined by the fixed order of its morphemes, this fixed order is a necessary requirement for morphological correspondence and it enters therefore as an essential part in its definition. In the sentence, on the contrary, the order of words may and may not be fixed. Hence it is impossible to postulate fixed order in the definition of syntactic correspondence which is established by the syntactic function of phonemically and morphologically corresponding morphs (markers) without any regard of word-order. Thus Lat. *alumnus magistrum venerat* 'the pupil venerates the master' is equally correspondent to Skr. *aśvo ratham vahati* and to Skr. *aśvo vahati ratham* 'the horse draws the chariot' although the order of the phonemically correspondent syntactic markers does not in both cases correspond equally.

Both morphological and syntactic correspondence are based on phonemic correspondence. But in the former the status of the phonemically correspondent strings as parts of words and their order with respect to the other parts of the word-forms are both relevant whereas in the latter both are irrelevant. In morphological correspondence the function of the phonemically correspondent strings remains unspecified, while in syntax they must belong to the expression of syntactic markers. Their precise morphological status is thereby irrelevant. The phonemically correspondent strings may in syntactic correspondence include more than the expression of the markers or only parts of it. Thus, for instance, the syntactically correspondent sentences Skr. *madhu pibati* 'he drinks mead' and OChSl. *nesetъ medъ* 'he carries honey' contain the phonemic correspondences *medhu* and *-et-*. The first of them contains much more than the expression of the syntactic marker *-u-Ø*, the second is only a part of the expression of a syntactic marker.

As has just been shown, there are criteria by which morphological and syntactic correspondence can, at least in principle, be clearly distinguished from each other.

6

THE CORRELATION OF REGULAR SOUND CHANGE
AND PHONEMIC CORRESPONDENCE

Regular sound change is the token by which we recognize genetic relationship. But regular sound change cannot be observed directly since it operates under conditions inaccessible to our perception. What we actually do perceive, is not regular sound change itself but the traces it lives on the languages derived by it. These traces consist in phonemic correspondences between the older and the younger stage of a language or between two or more younger stages of one and the same older language. Phonemic correspondence obtains between two languages if their phonemic strings are derivable from a common source by any number of sets of regular sound change rules. The common source may, of course, be identical with one of the languages compared. But even such an identity can as an identical transformation in cybernetics be subsumed under the concept of regular sound change. There is a close correlation between regular sound change and phonemic correspondence and the former can be recognized and its process reconstructed with the help of the latter. Phonemic correspondence bears witness of the regular sound change by which it came about. It offers the necessary data for the reconstruction of the sound change which determined the genetic relationship of language units and of languages. It will be our task now to investigate in more detail this correlation and to inquire into the possibilities it offers for the reconstruction of sound change.

It has been already said (chapter 4) that regular sound change can be expressed in the system of cybernetic concepts as an operator on which two important restrictions are imposed: on the left

side of the implications expressing the rules of the operator only
phonological data are admitted and on their right side no disjunctions are allowed. On the left side of the implications disjunctions
are freely admitted. A rule of transformation conforming to these
restrictions we call a sound law. The operator of sound change
is thus a set of sound laws.

The logic relation of implication is a convenient expression for
the rules of an operator. But they can find other equivalent expressions too. Mapping in set theory is quite equivalent to implication in logic. Thus the rules of an operator can be expressed
as a mapping of the operand on the transform. When sound laws
are being expressed in this way the mapped set will consist of
phonological items only and the mapping functions will be one-
to-one or many-to-one but not one-to-many or many-to-many.

The following implications can be accepted as the expression of
sound laws if we assume that o, p and q are phonological data:

$$(1) \rightarrow \quad p \ q$$
$$(2) \rightarrow \underline{y} \ o \ p \ q$$

whereas

$$(3) \rightarrow \quad o \ \underline{y} \ p \ q$$
$$(4) \rightarrow \underline{y} \ o \ p \ \underline{y} \ q \ r$$

must be rejected because they have on their right side a disjunction.

If we choose to express the same rules by the operation of
mapping, the functions will be as follows:

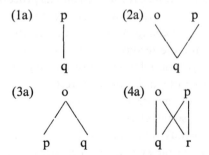

Here (1a) and (2a), which can alone be accepted as the expression of sound laws, have one to one and many to one functions, whereas the cases with one to many (3a) and many to many functions (4a) must be rejected.

So far it has been assumed that o and p are phonological items without further qualification. In fact, there are cases in which the sound laws cannot be stated for phonemes as such, but only for phonemes in certain phonological surroundings *i.e.*, for allophones. If two allophones of a phoneme are being transformed in a different way, we shall have a one to many mapping:

(5)

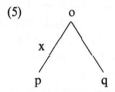

The x by which one of the functions is marked denotes the phonological conditions under which the transformation of o to p is operated, whereas under all other conditions o is transformed into q.

In such cases we have to do with sound laws because the mapping is not really one-to-many, as it may seem on first sight, but we have two one-to-one mappings

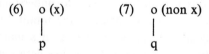

This conforms fully with our traditional usage since in such cases we speak of two and not of one sound law (*e.g.*, Grimm's and Verner's law).

We are accustomed to calling (2a) a merger and (5) a split. There are no real splits in sound change since the phonemic distinction that arises in the younger stage must have preexisted in the older one on a subphonemic level [cf. (4) and (5)]. The mergers are on the contrary very real since existing phonemic distinctions may disappear in sound change.

Allophones are no less phonological entities than phonemes and the existence of a phonological distinction is much more important than the level, phonemic or subphonemic, on which it manifests itself. In the latest development of linguistics there is a serious tendency to substitute a phonology of allophones for traditional phonemics.[1] The fact that sound laws can be exhaustively stated only in terms of allophones supports the views which stress their basic importance.

In the course of spontaneous sound change only mergers and no splits come about. This reveals a very important and quite essential trait of sound change: its ever-present tendency to destroy phonological distinctions. In sound change, the informativity of phonological items is constantly diminished. In fact sound change destroys language slowly and, if it was not for other factors in language change, regular sound change would end in making communication by language impossible.

It is this property which makes sound change irreversible and determines its direction. Of any two stages of language change we can tell by this irreversibility which one is the older and which the younger one. It is thus that sound change by diminishing the informativity of phonological items determines time and specifically linguistic time which can be measured by the corrosion effected by spontaneous sound change on phonological differentiation.

Having all this in mind, it is easy to understand why regular sound change has a specific place in the totality of the complex process of language change since it gives it a marked and easily recognizable direction and provides us thus with a useful criterion by which we can establish which language is to be regarded as an older stage and which as a younger one in the process of linguistic change. It allows us also to tell when two languages are not to be regarded as an older and a younger stage in language change but as two different younger stages of a non-attested older stage. In such a case our languages are the outcome of two different processes of sound change undergone by one and the same language.

Given the languages A and B, A will be regarded as the older stage of B, and B as the younger stage of A, if and only if the morphs of B can be derived from the morphs of A by an operator

[1] Cf. Chomsky (1964, 65 ff.).

which conforms to the requirements formulated for sound laws. A and B will be regarded as two younger stages of a non-attested older one if their morphs correspond phonemically but cannot be derived from each other by an operator which conforms to the requirements for sound laws. It is by these criteria that the descriptive statements of correspondence relations, as established in comparative linguistics, can be converted into historical statements.[2]

For this reason comparative linguistics is usually thought of as a historical and diachronic discipline, whereas in itself it is descriptive and achronic since its basic statements are such. Its results, however, can by the criteria mentioned above be transformed into historical and diachronic information. And it is for this aim that comparative studies are traditionally undertaken. Nevertheless, it is not correct to classify the comparative method as a diachronic procedure of research. In doing so we harm the clear understanding of what is done in linguistic research and obscure the correlation of descriptive and historical linguistics. The detrimental consequences of the failure to grasp the true nature of the comparative method have been gravely felt for some decades in the recent history of linguistics when it seemed for a while that a deep gulf separates comparative from descriptive linguistics, whereas it is not difficult to see that comparative linguistics not only presupposes description but also contributes very substantially to its completion by stating the interrelationships of the data obtained by the description of single languages. This being so, comparative research is not different in kind and scope from descriptive linguistics.

The sound laws can by definition be formulated only in terms of phonological units which in their turn have a certain distribution realized in the phonemic strings and in the suprasegmentals of the operand-language. This has as its consequence that the distribution of phonological entities in the younger language is wholly determined by the distribution of phonological entities in the older one. When a regular sound change represented by a one-to-one mapping (1a) takes place, the result is a phonemic correspondence

[2] Cf. Hoenigswald (1960b, 119ff.).

since the old and the new phonological entity appear always in the same surroundings. Of course, these surroundings can be called same only if we purposefully neglect the transformations to which they are subject by passing from the old language to the new one. But since these transformations also create correspondences as to the place of phonological entities in the strings, we can instead speak of correspondent surroundings.

The same happens when the morphs of two languages are derived from the morphs of a third one by two different sets of sound laws. Here again, the distribution of phonological entities in the two new languages is wholly determined by the distribution of phonological entities in the older one. Since every phonological entity in the younger language corresponds to such an entity in the older one, to every phonological entity in one of the younger languages corresponds by necessity such an entity in the other one, the relation of correspondence being transitive.

If a sound change expressed by a many-to-one mapping takes place, it results in more than one phonemic correspondence between the older language and the younger one. The number of these correspondences depends on the number of phonological items which underwent the same transition. If they are three as in

(8)   o   p   q
          \ | /
           r

they will result in three correspondences: o:r, p:r, q:r.

We shall turn now to the case of three languages, the morphs of two of them being derived from the morphs of the third by regular sound change. The older language we shall call A, the two younger ones B and C. We shall consider first the simplest case in which both sound changes are one-to-one mappings:

(9)   B   l
           |
       A   p
           |
       C   s

The comparison of B with C will in this case establish a phonemic correspondence l:s.

There are other, more complicated cases, in which one of the sound changes involved is a many-to-one mapping. The merger can occur in the transformation of A to B or in the transformation of A to C:

(10)　B　　l　　　　(11)　B　m　n
　　　　　／＼　　　　　　　　　｜　｜
　　　　A　o　p　　　　　　A　q　r
　　　　　｜　｜　　　　　　　　　＼／
　　　　C　s　t　　　　　　C　　u

A comparative examination of B and C will here yield two correspondences in each case: l:s and l:t in (10), m:u and n:u in (11).

Now we shall consider such cases where both sound changes are many-to-one mappings:

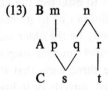

(12)　B　　m
　　　　　／＼
　　　　A　p　q
　　　　　＼／
　　　　C　　r

Here only one correspondence will be established by comparative research: m:r.

All more complicated mappings can be analysed as combinations of the cases mentioned above. So for example

(13)　B　m　　n
　　　　　｜　　／＼
　　　　A　p　q　r
　　　　　＼／　　｜
　　　　C　s　　t

can be regarded as (10) and (11) having two one-to-one mappings in common.

In all cases the number and the distribution of phonological entities in A is equal to the number and the distribution of the correspondences between the phonological entities in B and in C. The only exception is (12) where one correspondence stands for two phonological entities in A.

This analysis shows that there is a correlation between the possible types of regular sound change and the phonological correspondences between the languages involved in it. Therefore it is legitimate to try to reconstruct sound change with the help of the data provided by the establishment of phonological correspondences. But the aims of such an endeavour can be reached only with a high probability and never with absolute certainty since the interpretation of phonological correspondences in terms of sound change is not a problem that admits always only one solution. As we have already shown, duplicate one-to-one mapping (9) and duplicate merger (12) leave both only one phonological correspondence in the two younger stages. Duplicate merger is therefore irretrievable by the comparative method. This does not seriously diminish its value because of the low probability of multiplicate merger. The higher the number of parallel younger stages, the less probable it becomes that the same merger has occurred in all of them. It is because of this that the comparative method remains practicable in spite of its shortcomings.

We shall now consider the problem of two languages P and Q the genetic relationship of which is to be determined. We shall suppose first, for the sake of the argument, that between the morphs of P and those of Q phonological correspondences can be established. The genetic relationship of the morphemes of P and Q thus being proved, it remains to establish the kind of that relationship. There are three possibilities as to its nature: (1) P may be the older stage of Q, (2) Q may be the older stage of P and (3) both P and Q may be two parallel younger stages of a supposed language X. It is only in these three ways that P and Q can be genetically related, *i.e.*, connected, directly or indirectly, by regular sound change as expressed in sound laws.

In order to establish the kind of genetic relationship existing between P and Q, it is necessary to study their phonological correspondences. These can again in their turn be represented as

mappings of phonological entities of P on those of Q. As long as
we find only one-to-one correspondences of the type

$$(14) \quad P \quad l$$
$$| $$
$$Q \quad p$$

we shall interpret it as the result of a sound change of the type
(1a). There is no reason to assume two parallel sound changes as
in (9) and to postulate thus a third language X from which P and
Q are derived by different sets of sound rules. But it is impossible
to tell whether P or Q is the older stage from which the other is
derived by a sound law → l p or → p l.

For an illustration we shall take P to be Old-Church-Slavonic
and Q to be Serbo-Croatian. Between them phonological correspondences can be established and the genetic relationships of a
great many of their morphs cannot be questioned. It will be our
task now to determine the kind of this relationship. Among the
phonological correspondences of these languages there are many
which belong to the type (14). There are for example the correspondences $m:m$, $n:n$ and $e:e$. Cf. OS. *mene* 'me' and SCr. *mene*
'me'. In this case we have no reason to assume a third language
from which the OS. morph and the SCr. one should be derived.
But it is also impossible to tell which one of the two languages
is the older stage and which is the younger one.

When in the course of such an investigation one or more correspondences of the type

$$(15) \quad P \quad l \quad m$$
$$\diagdown \diagup$$
$$Q \quad p$$

are found, we shall interpret it as the result of a sound change of
the type (2a). There is no reason to assume two parallel sound
changes as in (9) and to postulate thus a third language X from
which P and Q are derived by different sets of sound rules. In
this case, as opposed to the precedent one, it is possible to determine that P is the older stage of Q since an operator transforming

Q into P would not conform to the requirements for sound laws (cf. p. 95ff), whereas an operator transforming P into Q would. Here we can state the sound law → y l m p.

Investigating the phonological correspondences of Old-Church-Slavonic and Serbo-Croatian many correspondences of the type (15) will be found. There are e.g., *u:u* and *ǫ:u*, *e:e* and *ę:e*, *ъ:a* and *ь:a*. Cf. OS. *uho* 'ear' and SCr. *uho* 'ear', OS. *rǫka* 'hand' and SCr. *ruka* 'hand', OS. *berǫ* 'I take' and SCr. *berem* 'I collect', OS. *męso* 'meat' and SCr. *meso* 'meat', OS. *sъnъ* 'sleap' and SCr. *san* 'sleep', OS. *dьnь* 'day' and SCr. *dan* 'day'. As long as there occur only correspondences of this type and of the preceding one, we must assume that Old-Church-Slavonic is an older stage of Serbo-Croatian.

If after the discovery of correspondences of the type (14) and (15) other correspondences occur belonging to type

(16) P   l
           /\
       Q p q

it becomes impossible to formulate an operator for the transformation of P into Q or of Q into P in accordance with the restrictions put on sound laws. In such a case neither of the languages can be regarded as the older stage of the other. Here a third language X must be postulated from which P and Q can be derived by sound laws:

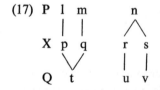

The number of phonological entities in X will be equal to the number of correspondences between P and Q, whereas the phonological entities of both P and Q are less than that number. The distribution of the entities in X can be established by the distribution of phonological correspondences between P and Q. Number and distribution of the phonological entities of X being thus known, it is necessary to look out for a language genetically related with P and Q which has the required number of phonemic entities in the expected distribution. If it can be found, we have an attested older stage of both P and Q.

Nevertheless, if the correspondences of type (15) and (16) established between P and Q are stated in terms of phonemes and not of positional allophones, it may still be possible to show that either P is the older stage of Q or Q of P. Phonemic split may occur in sound laws, it is only necessary to show that in one direction all splits are conditioned by phonological surroundings. In other words, if all splits from P to Q conform to the type (5) P can still be regarded as the older stage of Q. Although this criterion is very clear in theory, it arises many difficulties in practical application because analogical change of the distribution of morphs tends always to alter the original distribution of morphs (cf. p. 79 ff.). The distribution of phonological correspondences determining the splits is therefore only seldom to be found directly recorded in the material, but must be reconstructed by a procedure which rests on probability and hence gives no ultimate security, but always remains open to questioning and doubt. In many cases it is rather the intuition of the linguist than any firm evidence which determines how the conditioning of splits will be put and explained. A great many questions that remain open in historical phonology defy all attempts towards a satisfactory solution because no consensus can be achieved about the conditioning of phonemic splits. The evidence does not always point clearly enough in one direction.

We have shown already that among the phonological correspondences between Old-Church-Slavonic and Serbo-Croatian such can be found that belong to the types (14) and (15). If it were only for them, Old-Church-Slavonic could be regarded as an older stage of Serbo-Croatian. But there can be found also correspondences of the type (16). Such correspondences are *e.g.*, *št:ć, št:št, žd:d, žd:žd.* Cf. OS. *svěšta* 'candle': SCr. *svijeća* 'candle', OS. *puštati* 'leave': SCr. *puštati* 'leave', OS. *graždaninъ* 'citizen': SCr. *gradanin* 'citizen', OS. *dъždъ* 'rain': SCr. *dažd* 'rain'. As it is impossible to explain any of these one-to-many correspondences as a split conditioned by phonemic environment, neither of the languages compared can be regarded as an older stage of the other. A third language must be postulated which distinguishes such phonemic entities from which both Old-Church-Slavonic and Serbo-Croatian can be derived by sound laws. This postulated language is Proto-Slavic which distinguishes four entities where Old-Church-Slavonic distinguishes only two. In short, Proto-Slavic makes all the distinctions that occur in Old-Church-Slavonic and/or in Serbo-Croatian. A proto-language is thus a diasystem which makes it possible to describe simultaneously a set of languages.[3]

But not every diasystem can be interpreted as a proto-language. Such an interpretation is possible only for those diasystems which allow the formulation of one-to-one or many-to-one transformations by which the morphs of the languages, the simultaneous description of which is being attempted, can be derived from postulated morphs of the proto-language. It must be possible, at least in principle, to formulate such transformations for the content of the morphs also. In practice, however, this aim can only partly be achieved, since the description of linguistic content is, as yet, not formalized enough. This means that the phonemic units of a diasystem which can be interpreted as a proto-language must be set so as to account fully for the actual distributions of phonemic entities in the languages described.

Genetic relationship can thus be defined operationally as the possibility of constructing such a diasystem for a given set of languages. If it is possible to construct it, the languages are genetically related. If not, their genetic relationship cannot be proved. The diasystem is then interpreted as the description of a proto-language coded into the phonological correspondences between the related (cognate) languages. The correspondences themselves are ex-

---

[3]   Cf. Pulgram (1964, 376ff.).

plained as the result of regular sound change operating on supposed morphs of the proto-language.

It is usual to present this procedure as a method which enables
us to shed some light on linguistic prehistory and thus to complete
the data provided by the attested history of languages. This presentation of the methodological background of comparative linguistics overlooks, however, the most important fact that the device
sketched above is the only means to acquire ANY KNOWLEDGE on
language history, whether attested or not.

This statement is very much contrary to the common sense approach cultivated in traditional linguistic thought. We are mostly
inclined to believe that historical sources attest that Italian is a
younger stage of Latin, Modern Greek of Ancient Greek and
Modern English of Middle English. But it is not difficult to demonstrate that such information neither is nor can be drawn from
historical sources without the help of the comparative method.
What do the sources actually attest? They show that a language
was in use in a certain time at a certain place and in a certain
social community (cf. p. 32ff.). By their very nature they can
show nothing more since they consist of plain texts which can in
favorable circumstances be located in time, space and society. In
this way the sources can attest the replacement of languages in a
given space or in a given social community or in both. But they
never can attest in any direct way the genetical relationship existing
between the replacing and the replaced language.

Our sources attest quite reliably that in the communities of
Italy, where once Latin was in use, it was during the Middle Ages
replaced by Italian. But they do not, and cannot attest in what
relation Italian stands to Latin, whether they are related genetically
and how. There is no direct information about Italian being a
younger stage of Latin. Neither is there any information about
the alternative possibility that Italian has been brought to Italy
by the tribes we know to have invaded Italy during the great mi-
grations. And where such information exists, it may be quite un-
truthworthy as is the case with French which by its name is attested
to be the language of the Franks. It is only the comparative method

which shows beyond any doubt that it is a younger stage of the Latin of Gaulle.

It is easy to see that our sources cannot give any data supporting the latin origin of Italian in the sense in which they testify that Charlemagne was crowned Roman Emperor by the pope in 800 A.D. When we say that this fact is attested by the sources we presuppose that the writers of the sources and the modern historians have a set of concepts in common among which are: coronation, Roman Emperor, the pope and 800 A.D. or its equivalent in some other chronological system. If this were not so, the sources could testify nothing in the sense conveyed by the notion of historical evidence. The writers of the medieval sources and the modern linguists do evidently not share such common concepts as to the genetic classification of languages and hence the origin of Italian cannot be attested by the sources in the sense in which Charlemagne's coronation is.

But even if we choose to disregard this essential difference between political and linguistic history, there remains the inherent impossibility of establishing genetic relationship among languages by any other except the comparative method. The sources for linguistic history are texts and they contain only such linguistic data that concern the language in which the texts are organized. By their very nature they cannot offer data about its origin or its relationship to other languages. Such data can be provided only by a comparison of the language attested in sources with other languages attested in the same way. It is only by comparing Latin with Italian and by establishing their correspondences that the genetic relationship of these two languages can be known. Consequently, if it was possible for a person living in the early Middle Ages to find out and to record that Italian is a younger stage of Latin, he would necessarily have had to compare them first and this comparison would again be independent of and prior to historical recording. The process of Latin becoming Italian is in itself unaccessible to immediate observation and can therefore not be described in any terms translatable into our linguistic concepts.

Language being a discrete construct, its changes are necessarily replacements of one language by another (cf. chap. 3). But not all replacements are considered to be language changes. Therefore we distinguish internal and external linguistic change (cf. p. 35 ff.). Only internal change is relevant for genetic relationship. But it can be recognized only by the effects it has on the languages involved and by the correspondence relations it establishes. As a historical process it is by far too complex and to slow to be observed and recorded by contemporaries.

The difference between the Romance and the Slavic languages is consequently not, as often believed, that the origin of the former is attested whereas of the later it has to be reconstructed, the comparative method complementing thus attested language history. In both cases the same comparative method must be applied and a proto-language reconstructed. The only difference is that in the case of the Romance languages an attested language can be found which in all essentials conforms with the requirements put on Proto-Romance whereas for Proto-Slavic such a language could not be found.

But here again the difference is rather in degree than in kind, for, as Romance scholars know all too well, there is no absolute one-to-one correspondence between Proto-Romance and Latin, but these differences, although of the highest theoretical importance, can easily be neglected. The position of Old-Church-Slavonic among the Slavic languages is in fact very similar. It has a great many one-to-one correspondences with Proto-Slavic and is in practice very often used in its stead by Slavic scholars just as Latin is used as recorded Proto-Romance. Nevertheless, the differences between Old-Church-Slavonic and Proto-Slavic are greater than those between Latin and Proto-Romance and it is more difficult to disregard them.

It is essential to understand that every proto-language has to be reconstructed in order to find out whether any attested language can be considered to be identical with it. If a proto-language is found to be attested, this does not make the comparative method superfluous. On the contrary, it is only by the means of the comparative method that we can know that a language is a proto-language. Only after the work of reconstruction is done, we can decide if a proto-language is attested or not. In fact, this is the strongest possible argument in favor of linguistic reconstruction which has been exposed to many haughty criticisms. We cannot deny that reconstruction is possible and purposeful without asserting that historical linguistics as such is impossible or purposeless or both.

The implications of rejecting linguistic reconstruction go even further. As proto-languages are diasystems describing simultaneously the inventories and the distribution of units in a set of languages, those who reject not only the historical interpretation of such diasystems but consider even their setting up not to be an essential part of linguistic science, deprive themselves of a most powerful descriptive device and recognize only the full description of single languages as linguistic work of real importance. Such a linguistic science excludes from its field of study linguistic variety, one of the most important features of the linguistic phenomenon.

As could be shown, the correlation between regular sound change and the phonological correspondences it effects allows us to establish the sound changes that occurred in the past by interpreting the phonological correspondences among languages and to determine thus their genetic relationships. And yet many objections have been raised against the reconstruction of proto-languages. It is often believed that reconstructed proto-languages which cannot be identified with attested languages are not realistic enough to be of any relevance to linguistics. Although this attitude is evidently unjustified, as could be shown by pointing out that any historical work in linguistics presupposes reconstruction and that reconstruction must, consequently, be possible and tolerably realistic, the correlation between regular sound change and phonological correspondences is not tight enough to deprive this scepticism entirely of its justification. It is necessary therefore to consider the cases in which the information about sound changes which actually occurred is lost beyond any retrieval from the correspondence relations effected by it.

Duplicate merger

(18)

is a case where the actual sound change cannot be established by the information from the resulting correspondence m:s between the two younger stages. Hence (18) cannot be distinguished in reconstruction from (9) by comparing B with C and it is impossible to know that the proto-language actually distinguished two phonological entities where the compared younger stages have only one phonological correspondence. Thus in comparing Russian and Serbo-Croatian it would be quite impossible to know that the correspondence *u:u* e.g. in R. *uho* 'ear' : SCr. *uho* 'ear' and R. *ruka* 'hand' : SCr. *ruka* 'hand' came about by duplicate merger of two Proto-Slavic phonemes: *u* and *ǫ*. It is only by comparison with other Slavic languages that this fact can be established. Cf. OS. *uho* 'ear', *rǫka* 'hand' and Slovenian *uho* 'ear' and *roka* 'hand'.

Whenever we establish a correspondence of the type (14) we assume it to be effected by a sound change of the type (1a) or (9). There is always a possibility that we may have to do with a sound change of the type (18). Yet, the comparative method can be applied without hesitation in view of the fact that duplicate merger is indeed less probable than other types of sound change. The greater the number of cognate languages we compare, the lesser becomes the probability of multiple merger. In fact it is the relatively large number of Slavic, Romance, Germanic and Indo-European languages that gives to the reconstructions of their proto-languages a quite remarkable probability of being realistic to a quite satisfactory degree.[4]

The case with duplicate split is different, although here again the information about the sound change may in principle be irretrievably lost. A single duplicate split

---

[4]   About the realism of reconstructions cf. Pulgram (1959).

(19)

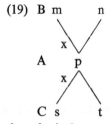

results in two phonological correspondences between B and C: m:s and n:t. It is their complementary distribution, the former occurring only in environment x, the latter only in other environments that betray the duplicate split and prevent us from interpreting the correspondences as the outcome of two sound changes of type (9). The distribution shows that the phonemic entities of the proto-language attested by the correspondences m:s and n:t were allophones and not phonemes. From these allophones the correspondences are derived in fact by two parallel sound changes of the type (9). The phonological entity designed in (19) by p must be a phoneme. Split is in sound laws possible only if they are stated in terms of phonemes. When they are stated in terms of allophones there can be no split. The phonemic entities of the proto-language reconstructed by the establishment of correspondences among the cognate languages are only allophones and they are to be classed into phonemes in order to reconstruct the phonemic system of the proto-language.

The real difficulties begin when there is not one but a whole series of duplicate splits sharing the same conditioning. As phonemic systems are integrated by correlations sharing distinctive features this possibility has a high probability of occurring. We have then

(20)

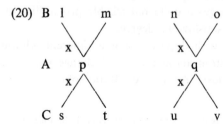

resulting in four phonological correspondences between B and C: l:s, m:t, n:u, o:v. Two of these correspondences: l:s and n:u occur only in the environment x whereas the remaining two: m:t and o:v appear only in other environments. Now it is impossible to proceed and to class the allophones, so established, into phonemes since nobody can tell which one of the two correspondences in one set is to be classed with which one in the other. This remains an impossibility only as long as we adhere to the algebraic notation used here. If algebraic symbols of phonological entities are replaced by real phonetic data it is the typological relatedness of allophones which in most cases allows us to classify them into phonemes in a satisfactory way.

The correspondences of French and Italian offer a case in question. Between these languages the following four phonological correspondences can be established among others: $s:č$, $ž:ǯ$, $k:k$, $g:g$. The former two occur only before correspondences containing front vowels, the rest in other environments. These environments can, of course, not be directly read from the French and Italian phonemic strings but have, as always in comparative linguistics, to be reconstructed first.

In other words, this is a realization of the correspondence relations we expect to be effected by sound change of the type (20). But here we have to do with full phonemic data instead of the abstract algebraic notation and therefore it is quite easy to classify the correspondences into original phonemes of the proto-language. The criterion is the typological relatedness of the phonemes that correspond to each other. In our case it is the distinctive feature of voicedness which makes the classification possible without a shade of doubt. Latin, as attested Proto-Romance, confirms fully such a reconstruction: the phonologic entities established by the correspondences are a palatal and a velar allophone of the Latin phonemes k and g. Because of such typological criteria, duplicate split is no unsurmountable obstacle for comparative linguistics.

Other difficulties arise when in regular sound change split is combined with duplicate merger. As a typical abstract example we can take

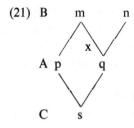

(21)

The result are two correspondences: m:s and n:s. The distribution of the former one equals both the distribution of original p and q in environment x. Since the differenciation of these two phonological entities of the proto-language is lost beyond any retrieval by the comparative method, it is only the distribution of the two correspondences that can be investigated. And in the distribution of these correspondences no trace is left of the original complementary distribution of the allophones of q. In this case information about the sound change is again lost beyond any retrieval. The loss of differentiation of some allophones in the proto-languages makes it impossible to classify them into phonemes with the help of the data provided by phonological correspondences. The proto-language distinguishes in our case three allophones: two of q and one of p. The correspondences inform us only about two phonological entities. One of them is an allophone of q and the other again an allophone of q and the only one of p. Knowing only these two entities it is impossible to reconstruct the phonemic system of the proto-language. The reconstruction remains here in terms of allophones and ignores the distinction of two of them.

An example of such an unfavorable correlation between sound change and the phonological correspondences it effects can be found in Greek and Osco-Umbrian. Between these languages the correspondences $p:p$ and $t:p$ can be established among others. Cf. *e.g.*, Gr. πῦρ 'fire' : Umbr. *pir* 'fire', Gr. πό-ϑεν 'where from' : Osc. *púd* 'what', Gr. τίς 'who' : Osc. *pid* 'what'. The distribution of these correspondences is not complementary, although that of $t:p$ is very restricted since it occurs only before correspondences

containing front vowels. Nevertheless, it would be quite impossible
to reconstruct the fragment of the phonemic system of the Indo-
European proto-language they represent where it not for the data
provided by comparison with other Indo-European languages.
Only in this broader context it can be shown that in Greek and
Osco-Umbrian a duplicate merger occurred between an Indo-
European phoneme and an allophone of another. Cf. Old-English
fȳr 'fire', Goth. *hvas* 'who' and *hvi-leiks* 'what like'. In such cases
the comparative method operates again on the assumption of un-
likeliness of multiplicate merger.

We have considered now the cases in which there is no one-to-
one correlation between phonological correspondences of parallel
younger stages and phonological entities in the proto-languages.
A number of factors could be discovered which may diminish the
realism of such reconstructions that cannot be checked by identification with attested languages:

1. Because of multiple merger distinctions between phonological entities in the proto-language may remain totally unknown.

2. Because of multiple split the allophones of the proto-language represented by phonological correspondences may become
difficult or even impossible to classify into the phonemes to which
they actually belonged.

3. Because of split combined with multiple merger it may become impossible to classify the phonological entities of the proto-
language as represented by correspondences into the original
hierarchy of phonemes and allophones.

The results of this investigation show that no reconstructed
phonemic system can be regarded as more than a hypothetical
approximation if no check by identification with an attested language is possible. The sceptical attitude toward the reconstruction
of proto-languages is in this sense fully justified. And yet the errors
coming from these sources inherent in the comparative method
are not very grave since the units of the reconstructed phonological
systems are always in a one-to-one or in a one-to-many correlation
with the phonological entities of the proto-language. The reconstructed system will always be A MODEL of the real one: Some dis-

tinctions will be neglected and some allophones will remain unclassified into phonemes. This model, however imperfect in some cases, will always give us a true if not a complete picture of the phonological system we try to decode from the phonological correspondences among genetically-related languages.[5] The data provided by the comparative method about the phonological system of the proto-language are quite pertinent and trustworthy, they must only be interpreted in the right way. In this far more important sense, the sceptical attitude towards the reconstruction of proto-languages is not justified.

The realism of reconstructed forms which has often been questioned does not depend exclusively on phonological reconstruction but also on morphological. The correlation of morphological change and morphological correspondences provides other sources of errors. They must, of course, be taken into account but they too preserve in any case a definite relation between the reconstructed morphological system and the real one of the proto-language. It is, first of all, the distribution of the morphs of the proto-language that may not be represented faithfully in the reconstructed model.

It is also important to note that it is not so much the realism of a reconstructed model of a proto-language as its historical interpretation that has raised many objections.[6] In this discussion generally no distinction has been made between the proto-language, its reconstructed model and the historical interpretation of this model. It was especially the absolute unity of the proto-language that was for many linguists and historians difficult to accept. However, this attitude is based on a fundamental misunderstanding. For it is not the real proto-language the absolute unity of which is being asserted but only the model of that proto-language. The model is a model of a set of languages which all share the properties expressed in the model but may differ as to other properties. It remains to be seen in every case of genetic relationship if the reality represented by the reconstructed model of the proto-

[5]   Cf. Katičić (1966a, 65ff.).
[6]   Cf. Katičić (1966a, 65ff.).

language was in fact a linguistic unity or a linguistic variety. It is necessary always to remember that what is reconstructed in comparative linguistics is a diasystem which can be interpreted historically.[7] The reconstructed model of a proto-language suggests absolute unity only because by definition it expresses the invariants of a variety. To understand it as a denial of that variety is to misunderstand it.

On the source of a genetic relationship there may be the spread of the language of a quite homogeneous social and ethnic group or a loose language league that came about by contact of speakers of different languages in similar conditions of life. In the first case there was much more linguistic unity and less variety at the outset than in the second. But whatever the unity was, it is it and nothing but it that can be reconstructed by the comparative method and that constitutes the proto-language in the technical sense of the term. The underlying historical reality has to be investigated in each case separately. Although data provided by the comparative method can be useful in such an investigation its methodology lies beyond the limits of comparative linguistics proper and should be made the subject of a separate monograph. What we want to stress here is that by reconstructing a proto-language nothing is said about the historical interpretation of the model and about how much variety is encompassed by its unity.

[7]   Cf. Pulgram (1964, 375 ff.).

GENETIC CLASSIFICATION OF LANGUAGES

The genetic relationship of languages is usually defined by sound laws: two phonemic strings are genetically related if one can be derived by sound laws from the other or both from a postulated third phonemic string. These three possibilities determine the three ways in which languages A and B can be genetically related:

$$(1) \quad A \qquad (2) \quad B \qquad (3) \quad X$$
$$\downarrow \qquad\qquad \downarrow \qquad\qquad \swarrow\searrow$$
$$B \qquad\qquad A \qquad\qquad A \ B$$

All cases of genetic relationship, however complicated they may be, can be reduced to combinations of these three basic patterns of genetic relationship.[1] Since derivation by sound laws is irreversible and points thus always in one direction, every set of genetically related languages is a partially ordered set in which some of its elements are ordered by the relation "is a younger stage of".

A partially ordered set whose all elements belong to a wholly ordered subset and in which every wholly ordered subset has an initial element is called a genealogical tree. It is easy to see that any set of languages containing only languages of a language family is in itself by necessity a genealogical tree. To draft such a tree on paper, as Schleicher and his followers did, is only an explicit statement of what is implicit in the very notion of genetic relationship among languages. In fact, it is impossible to reject the family tree as inadequate while still sticking to the concept of

---

[1]   Cf. Katičić (1966a, 62 ff.).

genetic relationship.[2] And yet many linguists have done precisely that in the last decades. Without being inclined to reject altogether the concept of genetic relationship among languages they have dismissed the family tree model with much indignation. It will be worth-while to inquire into the motivation of such a widely shared attitude which seems to have so little justification in the logical nature of the relations under study.

There seem to be two reasons which make it difficult for linguists to accept the genealogical tree as an adequate presentation of the genetic classification of languages. One of them is rather extra-linguistic while the other stands on purely linguistic ground.

For many linguists the genealogical tree is unacceptable because they fail to distinguish its logical nature, which models quite faithfully the existing relations from the historical interpretation of the model. They think that every knot of such a tree is to be taken as standing for a concrete historical people and every branch for an equally concrete and historical migration of an ethnic entity. Since it was difficult to accept such a mechanical view of the pre-historic events which brought about the genetic language families known from recorded texts, linguists were inclined to reject the family tree as naive and mechanical and tried to establish more sophisticated patterns which account better for what is known from other sources about the earliest history of ethnic groups. In doing so they did not realize that a genealogical tree as a model of genetic relationship among languages states only the abstract relations as presented in (1), (2) and (3) and that it leaves quite open the problem of how these relations are to be interpreted in terms of historical events.

Two identical family trees do not necessarily testify to two identical concrete historical processes. If Italian and Spanish are in the same relation of genetic relationship to Latin as German and Swedish are to Proto-Germanic, this does not mean that in both cases the same historical setting for the differentiation should be postulated. The possibility to use established genetic relationship among languages as a source for the reconstruction of historical

[2]   Cf. Katičić (1966a, 63ff.).

events is therefore much more restricted than we have learned to think. The other reason for the widespread reluctance to accept the genealogical tree as an adequate presentation of genetic relationships is the difficulty to apply it to languages as entities as opposed to phonemic strings and sets of phonemic strings. Sound laws as a criterion for genetic relationship apply by definition only to phonemic strings. To whole languages they can be applied only in so far as these can be presented as sets of phonemic strings. It is quite admissible to think of languages in that way, since a language can be defined as a set of sentences, and every sentence has its presentation in a phonemic string. The language itself is but a device for the mapping of a set of contents on a set of phonemic strings provided with the necessary suprasegmentals.[3] Sound laws can therefore be used as the basic criterion for the genetic classification of languages as entities.

This criterion, however, leads to a neat classification only of those phonemic strings to which the sound laws in question actually apply. Since all the phonemic strings of real languages never can be derived by a single set of sound laws from the phonemic strings of only one language, it is always impossible to classify a language genetically just by stating the sound laws by which its phonemic strings are derived from those of another. In every language there are subsets of phonemic strings defined by different sets of sound laws by which they are derived from other languages. The number of the sets of sound laws is not determined by the number of source languages. Phonemic strings of a language can be transformed by one or more sets of sound laws into phonemic strings of another language, each set of sound laws defining a different subset of genetically related phonemic strings. Cf. *e.g.*, the popular and the learned words in the Romance languages. Both are derived from Latin, but by different sets of sound laws.

Sound laws are operators transforming phonemic strings of the older stage into phonemic strings of the younger one. Practically, it never happens that all strings of the older stage are transformed into the younger one, neither does the younger stage ever consist

[3]   Cf. Chomsky (1964, 9 ff.).

only of strings transformed by a single set of sound laws from the older one. If it was not for that, historical linguistics would be the most economic description of the languages of a genetically related family. Instead of describing every language separately in full detail it would be sufficient to describe the proto-language and to state the sets of sound laws by which its phonemic strings are transformed into strings of the descendant languages. It would be necessary, of course, to add analogous operator rules for morphological and syntactic change.

And actually, such historical and comparative descriptions can be given, if not for related languages as entities, at least for their bigger or lesser fragments, while other fragments of the same languages remain outside the range of such descriptions. It is probably for that reason that recent descriptive linguistics remained unsensitive for the high importance of language history and comparative linguistics for the economic and efficient description of language families. The basic endeavour of descriptive linguistics was to get at the totality of language structure by using all accessible data without any exception. It is quite understandable that such a linguistic approach had no use for the description of fragments of languages, however effective, economic and integrated these descriptions might have been.

Things being as they are, it is, at least in principle, quite easy to classify genetically strings of phonemes and their subsets as defined by sound laws in a language. The classification of whole languages, however, calls for additional criteria and cannot be done on the basis of sound laws alone, since this criterion does not lead to neat and unambiguous results.

It is easy to demonstrate that *water*, *earth* and *fire* are to be classified genetically as Germanic. With equal certainty one can contend that *choice*, *voice* and *jury* are French and *limitation*, *agitation*, *serenity* Latin while *criterion* and *phenomenon* are Greek and *tea* Chinese. Every one of these subsets of English phonemic strings is genetically classified in a different way by the criterion of sound laws. After having taken notice of all such subsets it becomes less easy to say what is the origin of such a language as

English. Is it a Germanic language or a Romance one? If the last is true, there are again two possibilities. It may be a French dialect as *voice, choice, jury* and all other phonemic strings of their subset suggest, or an independent member of the Romance family, as *limitation, agitation, serenity* and their whole subset have to be classified.

If again we decide English to be a Germanic language, it remains to be settled whether it is a western or a northern one. *Egg, skin* and *skirt* with a whole subset of phonemic strings are to be classified as northern while *shirt, ship* and *shop* are western. It may be difficult to decide for a given phonemic string to which genetically defined subset it belongs, but this can be so only because the relevant data are not at our disposal and it is by no means a difficulty inherent in the principle of classification. The choice of a subset among all existing as the one which will be relevant for the genetic classification of the language as a whole with exclusion of all others cannot be done with sound laws alone since they give different results for a variety of subsets of phonemic strings which all together belong to the language in question.

We are used to take such a choice for granted and to speak accordingly of inherited and borrowed phonemic strings. From a genetic point of view we consider then the inherited elements to belong more intimately to the language than the borrowed ones do. But, taking this approach we are inclined to forget that the choice of what is to be regarded as inherited and what as borrowed has to be made. In other words, the language as a whole must be classified before we can know what is inherited and what borrowed. This selection cannot be done on the basis of sound laws because they point to all subsets of phonemic strings in the language alike. There is no inherent difference in the relations between *mother* and *mère*, and *choice* and *choix*, only the sound laws by which they can be derived from different hypothetical prototypes belong to different sets. They cannot BOTH define genetically English as such. An additional criterion is needed to tell which of them does and which does not. The established sound laws cannot by themselves offer this criterion.

If we try to present the genetic relationships of Modern English we must construct the following family tree in which every knot stands for a whole language and every branch for a transformation of phonemic strings by a single set of sound laws:

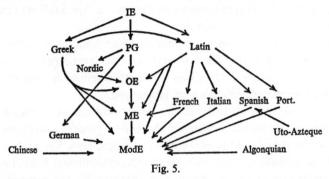

Fig. 5.

This highly complicated family tree presents only a fragment of the genetic affiliations of Modern English. Its purpose is not to exhaust the matter in any sense but rather to suggest its complicated intricacy.

To classify Modern English as a Germanic language independent of High German and Nordic means to accept as relevant for the genetic classification of that language only those transformations which are in our tree represented by vertical branches while disregarding all others as irrelevant. It is by such differentiation only that we get the well-known family tree:

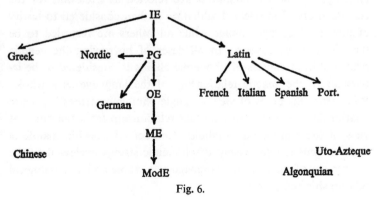

Fig. 6.

This family tree is derived from (4) by elimination of all branches which are considered to be irrelevant for the genetic classification of the languages which are represented by the knots in (4). Thus (5) presents the current genetic classification of the languages in question while (4) approximates to a certain extent a full statement of the actual genetic affiliations.

The genealogical tree (5) conforms to an additional restriction unobserved by (4): FROM THE ROOT OF THE TREE THERE IS ONLY ONE WAY TO EACH KNOT. This is a very essential feature of the current genetic classification of languages.

The relation of (5) to (4) shows clearly that our usual classification is not a simple picture of the actual genetic affiliations as shown by the possibility of constructing sound laws, but a selection of these affiliations conforming with certain significant restrictions. Most important of all information obtained by the comparison of (4) and (5) is the fact that our usual way to classify languages genetically implicitly contains two fundamental assumptions:

1.   Genetic classification of languages should be based on a selection from all existing genetic affiliations and

2.   For the genetic classification of a language only one of its genetic affiliations should be selected as relevant.

We can say, in other words, that the usual way of genetic classification is based on the selection of one affiliation (*i.e.*, transformation of phonemic strings by one set of sound laws) for each language. All other affiliations are rejected as irrelevant for the classification. The selected affiliation is then considered to testify of internal language change while all others are regarded to be the result of borrowing. In all cases of borrowing the genetic relationship of subsets of phonemic chains is considered to be irrelevant to the genetic relationship of the language as a whole. What from the point of view of single phonemic strings is genetic relationship, becomes thus contact relationship from the point of view of the language as a whole. Contact relationship manifests itself as genetic relationship of phonemic strings irrelevant to the genetic classification of the language as a whole and as typological relationship (cf. p. 24).

The two basic assumptions that could be shown to be implicit in current genetical classification make it possible to define with more precision the fundamental attitudes toward genetic classification. The traditional attitude of comparative linguistics accepts both assumptions. This amounts to the proposition: THERE ARE NO MIXED LANGUAGES. After any quantity of borrowing the language remains itself.

Against this prevailing view there was always an opposition making itself heard with contentions to the effect that THERE ARE MIXED LANGUAGES. Schuchardt and other opponents of the classical comparative grammar stressed this point very strongly. Such an attitude amounts to an acceptance of the first assumption and a rejection of the second. According to this view a choice has to be made among all the existing genetic affiliations of a language but there is no need to confine this choice only to one of them. There are cases in which a language as a whole can be classified in more than one genetically determined group.

A third most radical view maintains that ALL LANGUAGES ARE MIXED and that consequently all genetic classification is futile except the full statement of all genetic affiliations. Such an attitude appears in its purest form in the teachings of Marr. It amounts in fact to the rejection of both assumptions: There should be no selection of genetic affiliations at all. They are all equally relevant for the genetic classification of languages.

Since the two assumptions are not independent of each other, but the second presupposes the first, it is impossible to accept the latter while rejecting the former. There can consequently be no fourth attitude in the genetic classification of languages.

As we have seen now, the main controversies about genetic classification can be reduced to the questions whether there should be a selection from existing genetic affiliations and, if so, whether only one affiliation should be selected for the classification of every language. As all the alternatives sketched here are logically admissible operations on constructs, there is no way to answer the questions by deductive reasoning. In such a case the decision must remain arbitrary, except if it can be shown that one of the alternatives explains some feature of the empirical material under study which remains otherwise unexplained.

It is not difficult to show that the first question should be answered in the positive and that a selection among the existing affiliations should be made in genetic classification. The quantitative differences among the genetically defined subsets are, as experience shows, too great to be disregarded. These differences make it unadequate to consider all the affiliations as equally important for the genetic classification of a language as a whole. So it is impossible in the genetic classification of Modern English to give an equal importance to the subsets of phonemic strings transformed from Old English or from Norman French and to those transformed from Chinese or even Nordic.

A quick glance at the quantitative relations among the genetically-defined subsets of phonemic strings in Modern English shows that those derived from Old English and Norman French are so very much more numerous than the other ones that they must be granted a superior relevance in the genetic classification of that language. So if there are mixed languages, it will be most meaningful to classify Modern English as a mixed West Germanic and French language its other components being disregarded as irrelevant to this general classification. It is therefore preferable to accept the first assumption in order to make it possible to differentiate the basic genetic components of a language as opposed to subsets with a quite insignificant number of phonemic strings. The self-evident difference between West Germanic or French and the other sources from which Modern English phonemic strings are derived by sound laws show very well why it is important to provide for a selection of affiliations in any theory of the genetic classification of languages.

It is more difficult to answer the second question whether only one genetical affiliation should be selected as relevant in all cases. Modern English seems to present an argument against the acceptance of such an assumption since at first glance it is impossible to decide whether Old-English or Norman French should be selected. The quantitative criterion, so evidently pertinent in the answer to the first question, is of no use here. As long as more than one derivation may be selected as relevant for the classification of the language, the quantitative criteria can be applied in an adequate manner because all significantly more numerous subsets can be selected as relevant for the genetic classification of languages. There is no restriction on the selection that could prevent us from accepting all significant quantitative differences as criteria for the selection of relevant affiliations.

If we accept the restriction that only one derivation by a single set of sound laws may be selected, the whole situation changes immediately. Wherever there is more than one genetically-defined subset of phonemic strings exceeding by far in numerosity all the rest of such subsets taken together, we are forced to select one of these numerous subsets at the expense of the others even if there is no significant quantitative difference among them. Modern English is here a case in question. At first glance it is clear that the West-Germanic and the Norman French subset each outnumber very significantly the rest of the genetically-defined subsets. But between them there is no significant quantitative difference which could allow us to select on that basis one of them as relevant for the genetic classification of the Modern English language as a whole.

The question is whether in such cases there is any non-trivial criterion which can help us to make such a choice. If there is not, then there is no reason at all for such a choice and we must admit that languages can be mixed. The common view that there are no mixed languages can be upheld only if there is a criterion immanent in the linguistic data with the help of which the choice can be made between different genetically-defined subsets of phonemic strings in such cases where the quantitative relations are of no use. What is the linguistic reason to contend that Modern English is a younger stage of Old English which borrowed heavily from Norman French and not, on the contrary, a younger stage of Norman French which borrowed heavily from a younger stage of Old English?

It is obvious that the phonemic strings which serve as an expression to morphemes of different classes are not of the same relevancy for the genetic classification of languages as entities. As far as lexical morphemes are concerned it can be shown that different genetic affiliations have not an equal distribution among all the semantic classes of the vocabulary. There are semantic classes in which loan words are bound to appear more often than in others. Such an obvious class is composed by lexems denoting objects imported from foreign countries. Another consists of lexems refering to concepts of a foreign system of spiritual values. If one of two genetic derivations tends to be confined to such semantic classes whereas the other occurs everywhere through the vocabulary, it is easy to make the choice and to select the more universal genetic derivation as relevant for the genetic classification of the whole of the language.

In this sense a basic vocabulary can be distinguished from the rest of the lexical morphemes. It consists of such lexical units which are least likely to be borrowed. Although the attempts to state such a basic vocabulary were not crowned with much success until now despite many statements to the contrary,[4] it is clear that not all strata of the vocabulary are equally open to the intrusion of borrowings. We know intuitively very well this to be so, but it is not easy to find a methodologically sound criterion by which the borrowed and the inherited elements may be identified. In order to be able to know which semantic classes of lexical morphemes are most exposed to borrowing we must have an experience with languages in which the problem of selecting the inherited from the borrowed morphs has already been solved. But if we try to find a theoretically sound solution, we must find one which does not presuppose that in other cases the problem has already been solved. In order to achieve that we have only to consider the cases where the quantitative criterion gives an unambiguous answer to the question which genetically-defined subset is to be selected as relevant for the genetic classification of the language as a whole. In such languages the few borrowed morphs appear in always the same semantic classes of morphemes.

[4] Cf. Fodor (1965, 57 ff.).

It happens that these classes are exactly those which denote objects and ideas of foreign provenience, and they are just those which by deduction can be expected to be open to borrowings. Thus extralinguistic and linguistic considerations point in the same direction and give, at least in principle, the necessary criterion for the selection of one among all existing derivations as alone relevant for the genetic classification of languages as entities.

So it can be stated that verbs are less open to borrowed morphs than substantives are, and among the morphemes of both big classes there are quite clearly observable differences. Pronouns and numerals are still seldomer borrowed. The class which is least of all exposed to borrowing is composed by the grammatical morphemes. The morphs which serve as their expression are mostly homogeneous as to their origin. This holds true even in extreme cases of 'language mixture'.

An interesting example is furnished by the language of the city dwelling and highly urbanized Macedo-Rumanians in Bitola (Monastir) in the Yugoslav part of Macedonia. For generations these people feel themselves to be a part of the Greek nation. The older generation have all attended Greek schools. Their language for all manifestations of cultural and spiritual life is Greek. In the intimate circle of the family the parents of those who are now 70 spoke what they believed to be their separate language, namely Macedo-Rumanian. In this language many phonemic strings can be recognized which are genetically derived from Modern-Greek, others again from Latin, and these by sound laws similar to those by which Daco-Rumanian is derived from Latin.

It remains to be seen whether this peculiar language of the urbanized Macedo-Rumanians of Bitola is a Macedo-Rumanian dialect which has entered into very substantial contact relationship with Modern Greek or whether it is a modern Greek dialect with a strong contact relationship with the extinct Macedo-Rumanian of Bitola. Such a supposed extinction of the Macedo-Rumanian in highly urbanized Bitola does not contradict the fact that in less urbanized communities, especially among nomadizing pastors other Macedo-Rumanian dialects may be still in full use.

The question how the dialect of the Macedo-Rumanians of Bitola has to be classified genetically can be answered only by observing the distribution of the two genetic derivations in the different semantic classes of morphemes. Only if the distribution can be shown not to be equal, it will be meaningful to classify the language of the Macedo-Rumanians of Bitola either as Modern-Greek or as Macedo-Rumanian. If the distribution appears to be equal, the only meaningful conclusion will be that the ethnic group under observation speaks a mixed language.

In order to see whether even such a product of extreme language mixture can with good reason be classified as a real mixed language it was necessary to elicit some texts from qualified informants. A Macedo-Rumanian doctor, Mr. Anastasios Fila presented himself in that capacity. He was born and has grown up in Bitola in an urban family. He is now at the age of about 70. The language he learned first was that of his ethnic group. As most of the urban Macedo-Rumanians of his generation he went to Greek schools and got a thorough Greek education. Eager to explain in a conversation how very much greek their specific dialect in everyday talk was he quoted the following sentences:

(i) *Prospaϑiséku să lu katapisésku ma éste aδínaton.* 'I try to persuade him but it is impossible'.

(ii) *Erám la ipuryía i la nomarhía i la δimarhía ši det una anaforáe ši feč parápone.* 'I was at the ministery or at the district office or at the community office and I gave a report and I made some complaints'.

At first glance the mixture of Greek and Rumanian is evident. Both elements are so numerous that a quantitative difference arrived at by minute counting could never be accepted in good conscience as a criterion for the genetic classification of the language as a whole. But when a specification is made of the morphs which can be derived from Greek and of those which can be derived from Rumanian a quite characteristic distribution of both genetic affiliation appears.

From Greek can be derived:

prospaϑis	'to try'
katapis	'to persuade'
aδínaton	'impossible'
ipurγía	'ministery'
nomarhía	'district office'
δimarhía	'community office'
anaforá	'report'
parapon	'complaint'
i	'or' (if this is not the Arumanian *e* 'or').

All these morphs of Greek origin serve as the expression of full lexical morphemes.

The morphs of Rumanian origin are:

esku	'1 sg. pres.'
să	'that' (indicative conjunction)
lu	'him'
éste	'is'
erám	'I was'
la	'at'
ši	'and'
det	'I gave'
feč	'I made'
e	'nom. pl.' (in *parápone*)
e	'nominal suffix' (in *anaforáe* where it Arumanizes the word).

Only *ma* 'but' remains ambiguous. Its ultimate origin is Latin *magis* 'more' and it can be derived from Italian through Modern Greek to the dialect of the Macedo-Rumanians of Bitola. But at least the possibility must be considered that a parallel derivation has taken place in Macedo-Rumanian.

The morphs transformed by sound laws from Proto-Rumanian are mostly the expression of grammatical morphs or of conjunctions, pronouns and such lexical morphemes the content of which denotes structural items rather than objects of the outside world.

This inequality of the distribution gives us the possibility to classify the dialect under consideration as a Macedo-Rumanian dialect which has been exposed to strong influence of Modern Greek and has hence developed a close contact relationship with that language. The genetic affiliation of the morphs of grammatical and other structural morphemes including pronouns and some verbs are more relevant for the classification of the language as a whole than the morphs of full lexical morphemes.

Such an interpretation of the available data about the genetic affiliations of the language of the Arumanian community in Bitola is further strongly confirmed by the fact that in both *prospaθis*- and *katapis* a Greek grammatical morph marking these forms as belonging to the aorist stem is disregarded since the forms serve both as present stems. Furthermore, in *anaforáe* the greek *anaforá* is arumanized by a suffixal element *-e* which has the sole purpose to make the word conform with a rule of Arumanian phonology according to which no word can end in a stressed *a*. The morphs with Greek genetic affiliation have thus no connection with the Greek morphological system and they are subject to the restrictions of Arumanian phonology.

These considerations suggest additional criteria for the genetic classification of languages. It could, of course, be maintained that the language spoken in family by the urbanized Arumanians in Bitola is nevertheless Modern Greek which has undergone considerable morphological change and whose phonological system has developed a close typological relationship with that of Arumanian in course of a long and intimate contact. Although such an interpretation is obviously less satisfactory than the former one since the latter one involves more change than absolutely necessary, it can still not be entirely ruled out on purely theoretical grounds. Therefore the inequality of distribution of genetic affiliations of morphs belonging to different classes (lexical and structural) remains the only really conclusive basis for the genetic classifications of languages as entities as opposed to their fragments.

The validity of such a criterion of selection can be corroborated by quite general consideration. It is the content of full lexical

morphemes that can easiest be understood in an otherwise unknown language, whereas the content of the morphemes indicating
the structure cannot be understood without a knowledge of that
structure. To anybody foreign to the language the content of such
morphemes is of no interest at all. The basic situation underlying
linguistic borrowing can be expressed with the question "How do
you call this?" put by a foreigner to the speaker of a language. It
is difficult to imagine such a question asked about the content of
grammatical and other structural morphemes. It is therefore quite
natural that morphs of full lexical morphemes are much more
often borrowed than the morphs of structural morphemes and,
above all, grammatical ones.

Th. Magner quotes in his monograph on the Serbo-Croatian
dialect of Zagreb the sentence:

> (iii) *bedinerica klopfa tepihe v lihthofu.* 'the servant
> girl is beating the rugs in the courtyard'.

in order to illustrate the presence of many germanisms in the
dialect.[5] Again the question can be posed why we are so sure that
the language in question is a Serbo-Croatian dialect with German
borrowings and not a German dialect with Serbo-Croatian borrowings. Magner's quotation, although intended to show the
"German character" of the Zagreb dialect, gives by itself a pertinent answer. The morphs of all lexical morphemes in the text are
derived from German whereas the morphs of all grammatical
morphemes including prepositions are derived from Serbo-Croatian. It is the latter which are alone relevant for the classification
of the language as a whole. Here again language mixture led to
an unequal distribution of phonemic strings with various genetic
affiliations, and this unequal distribution calls for a differentiation
of the status of the German and the Serbo-Croatian morphs. The
differentiation is achieved by the distinction of borrowed and inherited morphs.

Here again history can give no additional criteria. From historical records we know that speakers of Macedo-Rumanian and

---

[5]   (1966, 12ff.).

Modern Greek in Bitola and of Serbo-Croatian and German in Zagreb came into close contact. But this is all information that history can give us. There are and there can be no records about which language prevailed in the community and who borrowed from whom. This we can know only by comparative linguistic research. History depends for this wholly on the genetic classification of the languages of the Macedo-Rumanian ethnic group in Bitola and the autochtonous population of Zagreb. It is clear that historical information can in no way help that classification except by providing texts which record the languages in question. The classification itself must be done by purely linguistic criteria.

In this preliminary sketch it was possible only to mark some evident tendencies and to show how our current genetic classification of languages finds in these tendencies its basic criteria. It will be necessary to investigate the distribution of morphs with different genetic affiliations in semantic classes of morphemes in full detail and on a large material including samples of a great many languages. Only after such a thorough investigation it will become possible to formulate general statements which will not be confined to most general tendencies.

But even as things are now, we can say that although nothing may be impossible in borrowing, the unequal distribution of morphs derived from different languages will as a strongly marked tendency most probably appear in all hitherto unexamined cases.

There is, however, another tendency which limits to a certain extent the realization of the other one described above. The nearer the genetical relationship of the languages from which morphs are derived by sound laws into morphs of a third one the less clear-cut will be the unequal distribution of the morphs of different origin in the morpheme classes of the third language. This is a fundamental reason why the genetic classification of dialects presents essentially greater difficulties than that of languages.[6] It is therefore easy to understand why dialectologists usually were most critical of the current assumptions about the genetic classification of languages.

[6]   Cf. Hockett (1958, 485 ff.).

Here again it is possible to find a rational explanation. When languages are closely related genetically, it is possible for a speaker of the one to identify and to understand the structural morphemes of the other. The things which prevent the borrowings of morphs of structural morphemes do not operate in such cases or they operate to a much lesser extent. But here again a big amount of dialectological research conducted from this point of view is necessary before we shall be able to make any general statement with more detail. Only on such a basis general criteria can be found which will help us to see clearer in the intricate matter of dialect classification.

If we accept the genetic relationship of the morphs of grammatical and other structural morphemes including pronouns and some verbs as relevant for the genetic classification of the language even such notoriously difficult cases as Modern English or Rumanian cease to be ambiguous. Even in the compound comparative of English adjectives, which was probably introduced under French influence, the structural morphemes are of Germanic origin. In a similar way Rumanian can be classified as a Romance language since the morphs of grammatical and other structural morphemes are in their vast majority derived from Latin by the sound laws characteristic for Rumanian. The traditional address heading prefaces

(iv)   *iubite citatorule*   'beloved reader'

is an example.

This investigation has shown, as we believe, that the current principles of genetic classification are sound and should remain in full use in spite of the severe criticisms to which they were exposed. There is ample reason to answer both fundamental questions put in this chapter in the positive: Among all the genetic affiliations of the phonemic strings of a language there should be a selection, and only one of all these transformations by which the phonemic strings are derived should be selected as relevant for the genetic classification of the language as a whole. The traditional view that there are no mixed languages seems thus to be fully justified.

Of course this does not mean that the assertion of the existence of mixed languages or even the opinion that all languages are mixed are to be rejected altogether as false. On the contrary, they are both true, but their truth is of a different hierarchical order than the truth that there are no mixed languages.

The proposition that all languages are mixed is true in the sense that there is practically no language in which all phonemic strings are transformed from only one language by a single set of sound laws. But this does not mean that all the genetically-defined subsets derived from different languages and/or by different sets of sound laws are all equally significant and that no other genetic classification of the language as a whole is possible than the full statement of its genetic affiliations.

The other proposition that there are mixed languages is true in the sense that there are languages in which more than one genetically-defined subset of phonemic strings is highly significant so that quantitative criteria do not allow the meaningful selection of one of them as more relevant than the other. But this does not mean that all such subsets are absolutely equal in relevancy and that no meaningful selection at all can be made among them. The inequality of their distribution in different classes provides a firm and objective criterion for such a selection.

The third proposition that there are no mixed languages is true because criteria can be found for such a classification. It seems to be possible to assign every language to one and only one derivation by sound laws from another language. Therefore no qualification of the truth of this proposition is needed. But this does not mean that all the other genetic affiliations which are not accepted as relevant for the classification of the language cease to exist. Therefore the contradicting propositions remain true in a sense which, of course, needs further qualification.

The traditional family tree introduced by Schleicher is thus an adequate model of presentation of the genetic relationship of languages. It is only illegitimate to interpret it automatically as a universal pattern of historical processes of ethnogenesis. Every time when a genealogical tree of related languages is established it has to be investigated separately by what historical events it was brought about. The model of genetic relationship does not in itself answer that question.

But there are still other objections to the family tree which are put forward as arguments for its rejection. These objections are based on the difficulties encountered by linguists who try to establish a classification into groups of genetically related languages at a level between the proto-language and the single languages or well-established subgroups. It is the well-known problem of eastern and western Romance or that of Italo-Celtic, Balto-Slavic, Balto-Slavo-Germanic and Greco-Italic.

It is an essential feature of the particular family tree established by Schleicher that it states very debatable and hotly debated genetic relationships among subsets of Indo-European languages. Most of these closer Indo-European relationships have been rejected since and the discussion of these questions showed how highly intricate these problems are.[7] The Indo-European language family consists of a set of groups such as the Indian, Iranian, Slavic, Baltic, Germanic, etc. So far the consensus is general. The difficulties begin with the question whether some of these groups can be derived from common proto-languages of a lower rank than the Indo-European proto-language itself.

So far, there is common consensus of the comparativists only about an Indo-Iranian subfamily. It is generally believed that an Indo-Iranian proto-language can be postulated between the Indo-European proto-language and the Indian and Iranian groups. Much less unanimous are the opinions of the comparativists about a Balto-Slavic proto-language and subfamily. Still more debated is a closer genetic relationship of Celtic and Italic with the exclusion of other Indo-European groups.[8]

To such attempts at clearcut classifications many linguists oppose more differentiated views stressing the existence of a very

---

[7]   Cf. Meillet (1950), Porzig (1954), Devoto (1961).
[8]   Cf. Georgiev (1958, 218 ff.).

complicated network of relationship among all Indo-European groups where everyone is linked by some distinctive features with each one of the others. Iranian is closer to Indian than to any other Indo-European group, and yet as far as the treatment of the Indo-European voiced aspirates is concerned, it is closer to Slavic, Baltic and Celtic than to Indian.[9]

This is the old controversy between Schleicher's *Stammbaum-theorie* and Schmidt's *Wellentheorie*. It is only important to point out that the theory of genealogical trees works quite well for the Indo-European language family and for a number of subfamilies as Germanic, Slavic, Indo-Iranian. The difficulties begin when other subfamilies are established. The wave theory gives here in so far a better solution as it permits us to state relations of closer relationship which do not mutually exclude themselves but allow us to classify a group differently in accordance with different distinctive features of relationship. These distinctive features of relationship, as *e.g.*, the treatment of Indo-European voiced aspirates or the occurrence of *m*-desinences in some cases of the plural or the occurrence of *r*-desinences in some verbal forms we shall call isoglosses since the wave theory is in its essential traits an approach analogous to that of linguistic geography.

In a certain sense the critics of genealogical trees are right when they say that the wave theory is nearer to reality, for it allows to state all existing isoglosses, whereas any attempt at the construction of a genealogical tree in Schleicher's sense presupposes a selection of relevant isoglosses. The rest must be dismissed as irrelevant. Thus the treatment of Indo-European voiced aspirates is neglected as irrelevant when Iranian is classed into Indo-Iranian instead of into Irano-Slavo-Balto-Celtic.

Here again it is the question of finding explicit and consistent criteria for the selection of relevant isoglosses which alone really matters. Those accepting and those rejecting the Balto-Slavic subfamily and its proto-language obviously do not use the same criteria for the selection of relevant isoglosses. Meillet has rightly

---

[9] Cf. Hoenigswald (1960b, 151 ff.).

stressed the importance of common innovations as a criterion for such a selection. But the question remains, how common innovation is to be distinguished from parallel innovation in already separated languages since the result of both is the same.

As long as only innovations are stated, common or divergent, no distinction can be made between real common innovations and parallel ones, for such a distinction presupposes the relevance of chronological data. When chronological data are introduced into this consideration, those common innovations will be called parallel which occurred after the languages to which they are common have already undergone some divergent innovation. According to Meillet, only those common innovations which occurred before any divergent innovations took place are relevant for the classification of genetically-related languages into subgroups. This criterion is valid in principle, but it is often very difficult to get at the necessary data of relative chronology.

In all cases of well-established subgroups, as in the Germanic or the Slavic one, there is in all members of the subgroups a great deal of conspicuous common innovations prior to any divergent change in the languages of the subgroups. In order to state all data concerning the classification of languages into subgroups of a language family, a special kind of family tree has been deviced which shows the relative chronology of the first divergent and the last common innovation in two or more languages.[10]

It is important to stress moreover that the original unity, the proto-language of the family from which on common divergent and parallel innovations are counted is in itself only a relative unity since it can contain unknown or even disregarded differentiations and divergent innovations. If it were not for Old-Church-Slavonic, all Slavic languages would have animate masculines with an accusative singular identical with the form of the genitive singular, while the unanimates would present an accusative singular identical with the form of the nominative singular. If by chance Old-Church-Slavonic was unknown this trait would be considered

---

[10]   Cf. Southworth (1964).

to be Proto-Slavic, although with the evidence now at hand it can be shown that this correspondence is in fact the result of a parallel innovation which occurred after the main Slavic subgroups: the southern, western and eastern one, were already well-differentiated by a series of divergent innovations. Old-Church-Slavonic is distinctly a South-Slavic language and yet it has not introduced the form of the genitive singular into the accusative singular of animate masculines.

When the chronological priority of a divergent innovation is unknown or purposefully disregarded, it becomes irrelevant for the classification into subgroups, the proto-language being a model of all correspondences without regard to chronology, whereas all divergences become the basis of subclassification. This disregard for chronology, often unavoidable for the lack of chronological data, is another unrealistic element in the construction of proto-languages. But proto-languages, thus constructed, are unrealistic only in the sense that they do not present the whole reality. The part of it they present is quite realistically presented. Proto-languages are hence unrealistic in the sense in which all models are.

When we compare Old-Indian *madhu*, Avestan *maδu* and Old-Church-Slavonic *medъ*, all meaning 'honey', it is evident that *maδu* is to be classified with *medъ* because of the medial consonant, with *madhu* because of the vowel of the first syllable. When we accept the existence of an Indo-Iranian subfamily, we dismiss the first isogloss as irrelevant and accept the second one as relevant, although there is no inherent difference in the nature of the two isoglosses.[11]

Here again, the obvious solution is a quantitative criterion. There are significantly more isoglosses linking Iranian to Indian than to Slavic. It is in this sense that a language or a language group can be defined as a bundle of isoglosses. In the age of structural linguistics this sounds quite unacceptable but the bundle of isoglosses is only a comparative definition of a language by its relationships to other languages as opposed to a definition as a knot in a genealogical tree.

[11]   Cf. Hoenigswald (1960b, 154f.).

The fundamental question is, how can bundles of isoglosses be reduced to knots on genealogical trees without arbitrary selections of isoglosses from the whole network that exists in reality. The problem is, in principle, identical with that of genetic classification in general. It must, first of all, be shown that such a reduction is desirable or even necessary. The desirability and necessity of such selections becomes obvious when we realize that we never know how many isoglosses must there be in a bundle. Here we stand helpless before the age-old problem of how many grains of wheat constitute a heap. A criterion must therefore be found by which certain agglomerations of isoglosses will be selected as relevant for language subgrouping whereas others must be disregarded.

In the network of isoglosses linking the members of a family of genetically-related languages some concentrations and correlations can be observed. But who is to say how many of them are sufficient to establish a closer genetic relationship? Some cases are, of course, obvious, but elsewhere the problem proves to be insoluble by quantitative criteria alone.

In itself the conversion of waves into a family tree poses no difficulties as long as there is no requirement that only one sequel of branches should lead from the root to every knot in the tree. A tree without that restriction is completely equivalent to a presentation in waves. It is only because this requirement was taken for granted and the distinction between the tree as an expression of genetic relationship and its historical interpretation fully neglected that the necessity was felt to discard the family tree concept altogether and to introduce the new metaphorical image of waves which does not allow an exact statement as easily.

In the classification of genetically related languages in subgroups, a tendency to use phonemic correspondence of the morphs of grammatical and other structural morphemes as the decisive criterion can again be observed. But in this case we have no clear distribution. Greek and Latin agree in having Indo-European -oi and -ai as desinences of the nominative plural of o- and a-stems respectively, and yet the Greco-Italic hypothesis has little chance to be universally accepted. The Italo-Celtic hypothesis has found more credit because the morphological correspondences of grammatical morphs between the Italic and the Celtic languages are more numerous. But they are not numerous enough to establish an Italo-Celtic subfamily beyond any doubt as the Indo-Iranian subfamily is established.

Having given priority of relevance to phonemic correspondences of grammatical morphemes, we face again all the difficulties inherent to quantitative criteria for the establishment of discrete units. It is precisely for that reason that the question of subfamilies in the Indo-European language family remains mostly unsolved until the present day. This is the already mentioned problem of genetic classification of closely related languages (cf. p. 134). The distribution of morphs of different origin does not show in such cases an unequal enough distribution to become the basis of an unambiguous classification.

In order to solve this problem in a satisfactory manner additional criteria must be found. Here we shall confine ourselves to point out some general properties of intermediate proto-languages of a lower rank.

If there is a language family consisting of the proto-language P and of three languages A, B, C the morphs of which are derived from P by sound laws, we can express this genetic relationship by the tree:

(6)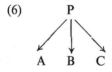

The sets of sound laws transforming the phonemic strings of P into those of A, B and C we shall call a, b, c respectively. These sets of operator rules define, when applied to P, the sets of phonemic strings of A, B and C. If the proto-language P is not recorded but reconstructed, it will contain as many phonological entities as are necessary for the most economic formulation of a, b and c. Thus, for example, all triplicate mergers will have as operand one single phonemic entity. This is a simple consequence of the fact that multiplicate merger is irretrievable in reconstruction.

It is always possible to construct a subordinate proto-language for any subset of {A, B, C}. Let such a subset be {A, B}. We can then construct its own proto-language P_1 and the diagram (6) will be transformed into

(7)

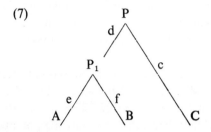

The subordinated proto-language P_1 is no new element in the diagram, for (7) is by definition equivalent to (6). In all cases where a and b contain identical rules they become in the new presentation rules of d. The rest of rules in d formulate identical transformations. Those rules which are different in a and b become in the new presentation rules of e and f respectively. The rest of rules in these operators are identical transformations of P_1 into A and B. Thus P_1 differs from P in all and only those features in which both A and B differ in the same way from P. In all other features: in those in which only A or only B or neither of them or every one of them in another way differ from P, in all these features P_1 is identical with P. By the construction of P_1 a and b are both divided into two parts. One is identical in both of them and the other is not. The rules identical in both are stated only once, in d, and they transform P into P_1. The non-identical parts of a and b constitute e and f and they transform P_1 into A and B. What in d, e, f is not covered by rules taken from a and b is provided for by operator rules defining identical transformations. Thus the construction of P_1 is nothing but a somewhat more redundant statement of what the presentation in (6) already contains. It just specifies what a and b have in common and in what they contrast. Therefore it is meaningful to construct P_1 only when a and b really have some operator rules in common. Otherwise d would consist only of identical transformation rules and P_1 would be identical with P and its construction purposeless.

When the results of the preceding analysis of most general relations is applied to our problem of subfamilies and proto-languages of a subordinated rank, it appears that an assumed subfamily with its proto-language may all to easily be a phantom: just a more redundant statement of what was already implicitly contained in the general statement of genetic relationship among the members of the family.

What we search for are criteria by which to decide whether such a subordinate proto-language and the subfamily it defines are to be interpreted as a historical reality. The commonly admitted criterion is a correlation between a relatively high number of non-identical rules in the operator transforming P into P_1 and morphological innovations consisting in analogical change. In other words, a significant number of isoglosses determined by an identical change process is required.

If we disregard the difficulty, ever-present in comparative linguistics, to state just how strong the correlation must be, how many non-identical transformation rules and how many common morphological innovations are to be regarded as significant, there is no reason why such a correlation should not be interpreted in historical terms. Such a subordinated proto-language can be the trace of a linguistic and historical reality. But we never should forget its constructive nature as exposed above.

In fact, what was said here about subordinated proto-languages of subfamilies applies to proto-languages in general when they cannot be identified with some recorded language and are thus established only by reconstruction. Such a proto-language is always a subordinated proto-language for the recorded members of the family which form a subset of the set of all members that ever existed. Such a reconstructed proto-language is therefore always a model of a reality and not the reality itself (cf. p. 115). And we can never tell by the model alone how faithful it is.

Every model by definition models a whole set of items, *i.e.*, all items homomorphous with the model.[12] This means that the linguistic reality of a proto-language may very well be a set of languages (dialects). The way such sets come into existence may also be different in different cases. It may be a set of dialects that came about through current differentiation of a language. It may also be an original language league with many borrowings, even of grammatical morphs, and a strong typological relationship developed through close contact.

Genetical relationship presupposes a (relative) unity in the past stable in the model of a proto-language. The statement of correspondences is therefore not enough for the assumption of a historical proto-language. Not every diasystem can be interpreted as a proto-language. The proto-language cannot be identical with the fragments of the languages compared that are derived from it. The operator rules by which the fragments of the languages are derived from the proto-language cannot describe only identical transformations.[13] For if they did, the supposed proto-language would in reality be only a very simple diasystem which cannot be interpreted historically. The proto-language is a maximal restriction of diversity at a point of time in the past. Disregarding this maximally restricted diversity we say that genetically related languages were once upon a time 'one single language'. Non-identical transformations reduce in every language the number of phonological entities and define thus linguistic time (cf. p. 98) and time depth is essential for the concepts of genetic relationship and proto-language.

It is not easy to find the criteria we search for and this theoretical reasoning is no attempt at a concrete solution. We tried, rather, to find out the true methodological nature of the approaches and procedures current in comparative linguistics to which it owes its remarkable successes and its apparent limitations. To understand what is actually done in a discipline may become the first step toward its being improved. But even if such hopes remain vain, it helps to integrate the empiry of that discipline into the general

[12] Cf. Katičić (1966a, 54).
[13] Cf. Katičić (1965).

theory of the science to which it belongs. The main purpose of this book is to integrate the traditional practice of comparative linguistics into the linguistic theory of our days by the attempt to formulate the basic assumptions of the former in terms of the latter.

Traditional comparative linguistics has often been criticized as foreign to the fundamental idea of structure its main interest being concentrated on the comparison of isolated words and forms. This sort of criticism can be shown to be based on one-sided approaches and gross misunderstandings.

The discovery by the *Junggrammatiker* of the importance of the assumption of regularity in sound change crowned the work of many decades of successful genetic research. The sound laws provide us with the only adequate method for the establishment of genetic relationship among languages. This implies that the languages in genetic research must be defined in the first place as sets of phonemic strings that serve as expression to certain contents. Such a definition contrasts, of course, strikingly with the definition of language in structural linguistics. Comparativists are consequently bound to search for correspondent phonemic strings dismissing their structural functions as irrelevant.[14] Such an approach seems really to contradict elementary structural principles and was bound to be considered foreign to the fundamental principles of modern linguistics. But this discrepancy is only apparent. For sound laws can be formulated only for phonological entities. They presuppose therefore structural description and have, in fact, anticipated phonology.

On the other side, the establishment of genetic relationship and the classification of phonemic strings and whole languages by that criterion is in itself a highly structural endeavour. As could be shown in this book, the transformations which express genetical relationship are for themselves a very complex structure indeed. This structure is essentially different from linguistic structure as investigated and presented in description only if the latter remains

---

[14] Typological comparison is on the contrary first of all concerned with structural function and was therefore much easier integrated into structural approaches and favored by their followers at the expense of genetic research.

strictly taxonomic in terms of item and arrangement.[15] But as soon as dynamic models in terms of item and process are applied in description, the two structures cease to be different in their logical nature.

It is at this point that our knowledge of linguistic phenomena has been much improved by the most recent developments in linguistic theory: the structure of language is one and the same with the structure of language change and genetic relationship. Although the descriptive and historical aspect in linguistic study remain distinct and must not be confounded, there is no difference in the very essence of the two structures and there is a definite correlation between the structure of the history of a language and the structure by which it functions as a code (cf. p. 82). It can therefore rightly be said that a language exists and functions by its history.

[15]   Cf. Hockett (1954).

BIBLIOGRAPHY

No attempt has been made in this bibliography to give a full list of works concerned with the topics touched upon in the preceding pages. It is intended to serve two purposes: to show the linguistic background of the theoretical ideas whose systematic presentation has been attempted in this treatise and to serve as a guide for further reading. As a matter of course, all works referred to directly in the notes are included. Further bibliographical information will be found in the works listed here. Fundamental works which are relevant to any inquiry into linguistic theory such as de Saussure's *Cours*, Sapir's and Bloomfield's *Language* and others are not to be found in this bibliography. It is obvious, that a book like the present one, must be based on their fundamental ideas and often refer to them.

Alighieri, Dante, *De vulgari eloquentia*, written in 1304-1307, first edited Paris 1577, Italian translation by Triffino (Vicenza, 1529).

Allen, W. S., "Relationship in Comparative Linguistics", *Transactions of the Philological Society 1953*, 52-112.

Austin, W. M., "Criteria for Phonemic Similarity", *Language*, 33 (1957), 553-568.

Bazell, C. E., *Linguistic Typology* (London, 1958).

Bechert, J., "Zur Geographie der Sprachtypen", *Münchener Studien zur Sprachwissenschaft*, 11 (1957), 46-48.

Benveniste, E., *Origines de la formation des noms en indo-européen* (Paris, 1935).

——, "La classification des langues", *Conférences de l'institut de linguistique de l'Université de Paris*, 11 (1952-1953), reprinted in *Problèmes de linguistique générale*.

——, "Problèmes sémantiques de la reconstruction", *Word*, 10 (1954), 251-264, reprinted in *Problèmes de linguistique générale*.

——, *Problèmes de la linguistique générale* (Paris, 1966).

Biggs, B., "Testing Intelligibility among Yuman Languages", *International Journal of American Linguistics*, 23 (1957), 57-62.

Birnbaum, H., and Puhvel, J. (ed.), *Ancient Indo-European Dialects* (Berkeley and Los Angeles, 1966).

Bloomfield, L., "Algonquian", *Linguistic Structures*, ed. H. Hoijer, 85-129.

Bonfante, G., "On Reconstruction and Linguistic Method", *Word*, 1 (1945), 83-94.

——, "Additional Notes on Reconstruction", *Word*, 2 (1946), 155-156.

Bopp, Fr., *Ueber das Conjugationssystem der Sanskritsprache in Vergleichung mit jenem der griechischen, lateinischen, persischen und germanischen Sprache* (Frankfurt, 1816).

Brockelmann, *Grundriss der vergleichenden Grammatik der semitischen Sprachen* I-II (Berlin, 1908-1913).

Brugmann, K., and Delbrück, B., *Grundriss der vergleichenden Grammatik der indogermanischen Sprachen*, I-II² (Strassburg, 1897-1911), und III-V (1893-1900).

Chao, Y. R., "Models in Linguistics and Models in General Logic, Methodology and Philosophy of Science", *Proceedings of the 1960 International Congress*, edited by E. Nagel, P. Suppes, A. Tarski (Stanford, 1962), 558-566.

Chomsky, N., *Syntactic Structures* ('s-Gravenhage, 1957).

——, "On the Notion 'Rule of Grammar'", *Proceedings of the Twelfth Symposium in Applied Mathematics*, 12 (1961), 6-24, reprinted in J. A. Fodor and J. J. Katz, *The Structure of Language* (Englewood Cliffs, New Jersey, 1964). Citations after this reprint.

——, *Current Issues in Linguistic Theory* (The Hague, 1964).

——, *Aspects of the theory of Syntax* (Cambridge, Mass., 1965).

——, *Cartesian Linguistics* (New York and London, 1966).

Chrétien, C. D., "The Quantitative Method for Determining Linguistic Relationship", *University of California Publications in Linguistics*, I, 2 (1943), 11-20.

Closs, E., "Diachronic Syntax and Generative Grammar", *Language*, 41 (1965), 402-415.

Collinder, B., "Jukagirisch und Uralisch", *Uppsala Universitets Årsskrift 1940:8* (Uppsala, 1940).

——, "La parenté linguistique et le calcul des probabilités", *Språkvetenskapliga Sällskapets i Uppsala Förhandlinger* (1946-1948), 1-24.

——, "Remarks on Linguistic Affinity", *Uralaltaische Jahrbücher*, 27 (1955), 1-6.

——, *Comparative Grammar of the Uralic Languages* (1960).

——, *Hat das Uralische Verwandte? Eine sprachvergleichende Untersuchung* (= *Acta Universitatis Upsalensis, Acta Societatis Linguisticae Upsalensis, Nova Series*, 1 : 4), (Uppsala, 1965).

Cuny, A., *Invitation à l'étude comparative des langues indo-européennes et des langues chamito-sémitiques* (Bordeaux, 1946).

Dante Alighieri, *vide* Alighieri.

Dempwolff, D., *Vergleichende Lautlehre des Austronesischen Wortschatzes* (Berlin, 1934-1938).

Devoto, G., *Origini indeuropee* (Firenze, 1961).

Diebold Jr., A. R., "Determining the Centers of Dispersal of Language Groups", *International Journal of American Linguistics*, 26 (1960), 1-10.

Dolgopol'skij, A. B., "Metody rekonstrukcii obščeindoevropejskogo jazyka i sibiroevropskaja gipoteza", *Etimologija 1964* (Moskva, 1965).

Doroszewski, W., "Dialektologija i sravnitel'no-istoričeskij metod v jazykoznanii", *Voprosy Jazykoznanija*, 5 (1956), 68-73.

Dyen, I., "Language Distribution and Migration Theory", *Language*, 32(1956), 611-626.
——, "The Lexicostatistically Determined Relationship of a Language Group", *International Journal of American Linguistics*, 28 (1962), 153-161.
——, "Why Phonetic Change is Regular", *Language*, 39 (1963), 631-637.
Ellegård, A., "Statistical Measurement of Linguistic Relationship", *Language*, 35 (1959), 131-156.
Ellis, J., *Towards a General Comparative Linguistics* (The Hague, 1966).
Fodor, I., *The Rate of Linguistic Change* (The Hague, 1965).
Fokos-Fuchs, D. R., *Rolle der Syntax in der Frage nach Sprachverwandtschaft* (= *Ural-altaische Bibliothek*, 11), (Wiesbaden, 1962).
Fourquet, J., "Pourquoi les lois phonétiques sont sans exception", *Proceedings of the Ninth International Congress of Linguists* (The Hague, 1964), 638-649.
Francescato, G., "Systèmes coexistants ou systèmes diachroniques", *Neophilologus*, 45 (1961), 37-44.
Georgiev, V., *Issledovanija po sravnitel'no-istoričeskomu jazykoznaniju* (Moskva, 1958).
Gleason, H. A., *An Introduction to Descriptive Linguistics*, revised edition (New York, 1965).
Greenberg, J. H., *Studies in African Linguistic Classification* (New Haven, 1955).
——, "The Measure of Linguistic Diversity", *Language*, 32 (1956), 109-115.
——, "The Nature and Uses of Linguistic Typologies", *International Journal of American Linguistics*, 23 (1957), 2ff. [a].
——, *Essays in Linguistics* (Chicago, 1957). [b].
——, "A Quantitative Approach to the Morphological Typology of Language", *International Journal of American Linguistics*, 26 (1960), 178-194.
——, *Universals of Language* (The Hague, 1965).
—— (ed.), *Universals of Language*[2] (Cambridge, Mass., 1963).
Gronke, E., "A Criterion of Relationship between Languages?", *Zeitschrift für Anglistik und Amerikanistik*, 4 (1956), 484-487.
Groot, A. W. de, "Structural Linguistics and Phonetic Law", *Lingua*, 1 (1948), 175-208.
Güntert, H., *Grundfragen der Sprachwissenschaft* (Leipzig, 1925).
Hall Jr., R., "The Genetic Relationships of Haitan Creole", *Ricerche linguistiche*, 1 (1950), 194-203. [a].
——, "The Reconstruction of Proto-Romance", *Language*, 26 (1950), 6-27. [b].
——, "On Realism in Reconstruction", *Language*, 36 (1960), 203-206.
Halle, M., "Phonology in Generative Grammar", *Word*, 18 (1962), 54-72, reprinted in Fodor and Katz (ed.), *The Structure of Language* (Englewood Cliffs, New Jersey, 1964), 334-352.
Hamp, E. P., "Morphological Correspondences in Cornish and Breton", *The Journal of Celtic Studies*, 2 (1953), 5-24.
——, "Protopopoloca Internal Relationships", *International Journal of American Linguistics*, 24 (1958), 150-153.
Harris, Z. S., *Methods in Structural Linguistics* (Chicago, 1951).
Hartmann, P., "Modellbildungen in der Sprachwissenschaft", *Studium Generale*, 18,6 (1965), 364-379.

Haudricourt, A. G., "Comment reconstruire le chinois archaïque", *Word*, 10 (1954), 351-364.

Hirt, H., *Indogermanische Grammatik*, I-VII (Heidelberg, 1927-1937).

Hjelmslev, L., *Prolegomena to a Theory of Language* (Baltimore, 1953).

Hockett, Ch. F., "Implications of Bloomfields Algonquian Studies", *Language*, 24 (1948), 117-131, reprinted in Joos (ed.), *Readings in Linguistics*, 281-289.

———, "Two Models of Grammatical Description", *Word*, 10 (1954), 210-234.

———, *A Course in Modern Linguistics* (New York, 1958).

———, "Sound Change", *Language*, 41 (1965), 185-204.

Hoenigswald, H., "Internal Reconstruction", *Studies in Linguistics*, 2 (1943), 78-87.

———, "Sound Change and Linguistic Structure", *Language*, 22 (1946), 138-143.

———, "The Principal Step in Comparative Grammar", *Language*, 26 (1950), 357-364.

———, "The Phonology of Dialect Borrowing", *Studies in Linguistics*, 10 (1952), 1-5.

———, "Some Uses of Nothing", *Language*, 35 (1959), 409-420.

———, "Phonetic Similarity in Internal Reconstruction", *Language*, 36 (1960), 191-192. [a].

———, *Language Change and Linguistic Reconstruction* (Chicago, 1960). [b].

———, "Allophones, Allomorphs and Conditioned Change", *Proceedings of the Ninth International Congress of Linguists* (The Hague, 1964), 645ff.

———, "Criteria for the Subgrouping of Languages", Birnbaum and Puhvel (1966), 1-12.

Hoijer, H., *Linguistic Structures of Native America* (New York, 1946).

———, "Linguistic and Cultural Change", *Language*, 24 (1948), 33ꞓ 145.

Householder, Fr. W., "First Thoughts on Syntactic Indices", *International Journal of American Linguistics*, 26 (1960), 195-197.

Isenberg, H., Diachronische Syntax und die logische Struktur einer Theorie des Sprachwandels", *Studia Grammatica*, V, *Syntaktische Studien* (Berlin, 1965), 133-168.

Ivanov, V. V., *Genealogičeskaja Klassifikacija jazykov i ponjatie jazykovogo rodstva* (Moskva, 1954).

———, "Tipologija i sravnitel'no-istoričeskoe jazykoznanie", *Voprosy jazykoznanija*, 7,5 (1958), 34-43.

———, *Obščeindoevropejskaja, praslavjanskaja i anatoličeskaja jazykovye sistemy* (Moskva, 1965).

Jakobson, R., "Typological Studies and their Contribution to Historical Comparative linguistics", *Proceedings of the 8th International Congress of Linguists* (Oslo, 1958).

Jarceva, V. N., "Problema vydelenija zaimstvovannyh elementov pri rekonstrukcii sravnitel'no-istoričeskogo sintaksisa rodstvennyh jazykov", *Voprosy jazykoznanija*, 5 (1956), 3-14.

Joos, M., (ed.), *Readings in Linguistics* (Washington, D.C., 1957).

Katičić, R., "Discussion of A. Capell's paper 'Oceanic linguistics today'", *Current Anthropology*, 6 (1965), 221-222.

———, "Modellbegriffe in der vergleichenden Sprachwissenschaft", *Kratylos*, 11 (1966), 49-67. [a].

——, "Der Entsprechungsbegriff in der vergleichenden Laut- und Formenlehre", *Indogermanische Forschungen*, 71 (1966), 203-220. [b].

Katz, J. J., and Fodor, J. A., "The Structure of a Semantic Theory", *Language*, 39 (1963), 170-210, reprinted in Fodor and Katz (ed.), *The Structure of Language* (Englewood Cliffs, New Jersey, 1964), 479-518.

Katz, J. J., "Mentalism in Linguistics", *Language*, 40 (1964), 124-137.

Katz, J. J., and Postal, P. M., *An Integrated Theory of Linguistic Description* (Cambridge, Mass., 1964).

Keyser, S. J., "Review of Hans Kurath and Raven I. Mc. David, *The Pronunciation of English in the Atlantic States*", *Language*, 39 (1963), 303-316.

Klima, E. S., "Relatedness between Grammatical Systems", *Language*, 40 (1964), 1-20.

Knabe, G. S., "O primenenii sravnitel'no-istoričeskogo metoda v sintaksise", *Voprosy jazykoznanija*, 5 (1956), 76-85.

Koppelmann, H. L., "Sprachmischung und Urverwandtschaft", *Album Boader*, 15-26, *Anthropos*, 37-40, 341-342 (réd.), *Anthropos*, 37-40, 889-890, H. Kähler.

Kroeber, A. L., "Statistics, Indo-European and Taxonomy", *Language*, 36 (1960), 1-21.

——, "On Typological Indices, I, "Ranking of Languages", *International Journal of American Linguistics*, 26 (1960), 171-177.

Kronasser, H., *Handbuch der Semasiologie* (Heidelberg, 1952).

Kuryłowicz, J., *The Inflectional Categories of Indo-European* (Heidelberg, 1964).

Lackner, J. A., and Rowe, J. H., "Morphological Similarity as a Criterion of Genetic Relationship between Languages", *American Anthropologist*, 57 (1955), 126-129.

Ladd, Ch. A., "The Nature of Sound Change", *Proceedings of the Ninth Congress of Linguists* (The Hague, 1964), 650-657.

Lehmann, W. P., *Historical Linguistics, an Introduction* (New York, 1962).

Lieberson, S., "An Extension of Greenberg's Linguistic Diversity Measures", *Language*, 40 (1964), 526-531.

Lohmann, J., *Gemeinitalisch und Uritalisch (ein Beitrag zur sprachwissenschaftlichen Methodenlehre)*, *Lexis*, 3 (1953), 169-217.

Ludwig, A. J., and Michalek, J., *Das Verwandtschaftsverhältniss der Sprachen* (Wien, 1946).

Magner, Th. F., *A Zagreb Kajkavian Dialect* (= *Penn State Studies*, 18), (Pennsylvania, 1966).

Malkiel, Y., "Language History and Historical Linguistics", *Romance Philology*, 7 (1953-1954), 65-76.

——, "A Tentative Typology of Etymological Studies", *International Journal of American Linguistics*, 23 (1957), 1-17.

——, "Paradigmatic Resistance to Sound Change", *Language*, 36 (1960), 281-346.

Marchand, J. W., "Was there ever a Uniform Proto-Indo-European", *Orbis*, 4 (1955), 428-431.

——, "Internal Reconstruction of Phonemic Split", *Language*, 32 (1956), 245-253.

Martinet, A., *Économie des changements phonétiques: Traité de phonologie diachronique* (Berne, 1955).

——, *Éléments de linguistique générale* (Paris, 1960).

Matveeva-Isaeva, L. V., "Sravnitel'no-istoričeskoe issledovanie rodstvennyh jazykov", *Učenye zapiski Leningradskogo pedagogičeskogo instituta*, 92 (1954), 9-34.

Meillet, A., *La méthode comparative en linguistique historique* (Oslo, 1925).

——, *Introduction à l'étude comparée des langues indo-européennes*[8] (Paris, 1937).

——, *Les dialectes indo-européens*, second printing (Paris, 1950).

Meillet, A., and Cohen, M., *Les langues du monde*[2] (Paris, 1952).

Menzerath, P., "Typology of Languages", *Journal of the Acoustical Society of America*, 22 (1950), 698-701.

Michel, L., *La dialectologie et la sociologie* (Louvain, 1937).

Milewski, T., "*Rozmieszczenie języków w czasie i przestrzeni* (=*Sprawozdania z czyności i posiedeń Polskiej Akademii Nauk i Umiejętności, Kraków*, 45), (1939-1944).

——, "Le problème des lois en linguistique générale", *Lingua Posnaniensis*, 6 (1957), 120-136.

——, "Predposylki tipologičeskogo jazykoznanija", *Issledovanija po strukturnoj tipologii* (Moskva, 1963), 3-31.

Moulton, W. G., "The Short Vowel Systems of Northern Switzerland", *Word*, 16 (1960), 155-182.

Osthoff, H., and Brugmann, K., *Morphologische Untersuchungen*, I (Leipzig, 1878).

Otkupščikov, Ju. V., *Iz istorii indoevropejskogo slovoobrazovanija* (Leningrad, 1967).

Paul, H., *Prinzipien der Sprachgeschichte*[4] (Halle, 1909).

Penzel, H., "The Evidence for Phonemic Changes", *Studies Presented to Joshua Whatmough on his Sixtieth Birthday* (The Hague, 1957), 193-208.

Pike, K. L., *Axioms and Procedures for Reconstructions in Comparative linguistics: An Experimental Syllabus* (Glendale, California, Summer Institute of Linguistics, 1950), mimeographed.

Polák, V., "Problém indoevropského prajazyka se stanoviska jazykové interference", *Slovo a Slovesnost*, 9 (1943), 56ff.

——, "K t.zv. indoevropskému problému", *Česky časopis filologický*, 3 (1944-1945), 133-134.

Polomé, E., "Zum heutigen Stand der Laryngaltheorie", *Revue belge de philologie et d'histoire*, 30 (1952), 444-471, 1041-1052.

Porzig, W., *Die Gliederung des indogermanischen Sprachgebiets* (Heidelberg, 1954).

Pulgram, E., "Family Tree, Wave Theory, and Dialectology", *Orbis*, 2 (1953), 67-72.

——, "Proto-Indo-European Reality and Reconstruction", *Language*, 35(1959), 421-426.

——, "The Nature and Use of Proto-Languages", *Lingua*, 10 (1961), 18-37.

——, "Proto-Languages as Proto-Diasystems: Proto-Romance", *Word*, 20 (1964), 373-383.

Ravila, P., "Die Ursprache als Grundbegriff der Sprachgeschichte", *Journal de la Société Finno-ougrienne*, 60 (1958), 3-15.

154

BIBLIOGRAPHY

Rogger, K., *Vom Wesen des Lautwandels* (Leipzig-Paris, 1934).
Ross, A. S. C., *Etymology* (London, 1958).
Ross Ashby, W., *An Introduction to Cybernetics* (London, 1956), reprinted as paperback (New York, 1963). Quotations after the latter edition.
Sandfeld, K., *Linguistique Balkanique* (Paris, 1930).
Saporta, S., "Methodological Considerations Regarding a Statistical Approach to Typologies", *International Journal of American Linguistics*, 23 (1957), 109-113.
——, "Ordered Rules, Dialect Differences, and Historical Processes", *Language*, 41 (1965), 218-224.
Šaumjan, S. K., *Problemy teoretičeskoj fonologii* (Moskva, 1962).
——, *Strukturnaja lingvistika* (Moskva, 1965).
Schlegel, F. v., *Ueber die Sprache und Weisheit der Indier: Ein Beitrag zur Begründung der Altertumskunde* (Heidelberg, 1808).
Schleicher, A., *Linguistische Untersuchungen* (Bonn, 1850).
——, *Zur Morphologie der Sprache* (= *Mémoires de l'Académie Impériale des Sciences de St. Pétersbourg*, VIIᵉ série, tome I, no. 7), (St. Pétersbourg, 1859).
——, *Compendium der vergleichenden Grammatik der indogermanischen Sprachen* (Weimar, 1861-1862).
——, *Die Darwinsche Theorie und die Sprachwissenschaft*[3] (Weimar, 1873).
Schmidt, J., *Die Verwandtschaftsverhältnisse der indogermanischen Sprachen* (Weimar, 1872).
Schönfelder, K. H., "Zur Theorie der Sprachmischung, der Mischsprachen und des Sprachwandels", *Wissenschaftliche Zeitschrift der Karl Marx Universität*, 2 (Leipzig, 1952-1953), 379-400.
——, *Probleme der Völker- und Sprachmischung* (Halle, 1956).
Schuchardt, H., *Slawo-Deutsches und Slawo-Italienisches* (Graz, 1884).
——, *Ueber die Lautgesetze: Gegen die Junggrammatiker* (Berlin, 1885).
Seiler, H., "On Paradigmatic and Syntagmatic Similarity", *Lingua*, 18 (1967), 35-76.
Senn, A., "Die Beziehungen des Baltischen zum Slavischen und Germanischen", *Kuhns Zeitschrift*, 71 (1953), 162-188.
Sieberer, A , *Lautwandel und seine Triebkräfte* (Wien, 1958).
Šimko, J., "On some Questions Concerning the Relationship of Grammar and Vocabulary", *Zeitschrift für Anglistik und Amerikanistik*, 3 (1955), 305-314.
——, "A Criterion of Relationship between Languages", *Zeitschrift für Anglistik und Amerikanistik*, 5 (1957), 191-199.
Skalička, V., "Problém jazýkove různosti", *Slovo a Slovesnost*, 10 (1947), 80-95.
——, "Tipologija i toždestvennost' jazykov", *Issledovanija po strukturnoj tipologii* (Moskva, 1963), 32-34.
Smalley, W. A., "Finding out how Close Related Dialects are", *Bible Translator*, 8 (1957), 68-74.
Sommerfelt, A., "External versus Internal Factors in the Development of Language", *Norsk Tidskrift for Sprogvetenskab*, 19 (1960), 296-315.
——, "Mixed Languages versus Remodelled Languages", *Norsk Tidskrift for Sprogvetenskab*, 19 (1960), 283-293.
Southworth, F. C., "Family-Tree Diagrams", *Language*, 40 (1964), 557-565.

Stankiewicz, E., "On Discreteness and Continuity in Structural Dialectology", *Word*, 13 (1957), 44-59.

Stevick, R. D., "The Biological Model and Historical Linguistics", *Language*, 39 (1963), 159-169.

Sturtevant, E. H., "The Pronoun *so *sā *tod and the Indo-Hittite Hypothesis", *Language*, 15 (1939), 11-19.

——, *Linguistic Change: An Introduction to the Historical Study of Language* (Chicago, 1961).

Swadesh, M., "Perspectives and Problems of Amerindian Comparative Linguistics", *Word*, 10 (1954), 306-332.

Szemerényi, O., "The Problem of Balto-Slav Unity", *Kratylos*, 2 (1957), 97-123.

Teeter, K. V., "Lexicostatistics and Genetic Relationship", *Language*, 39 (1963), 638-648.

Terracini, B. A., "L'héritage de la méthode comparative", *Acta Linguistica*, 2 (1941), 1-22.

Thieme, P., *Die Heimat der indogermanischen Gemeinsprache* (Wiesbaden, 1954).

Toporov, V. N., "O nekotoryh teoretičeskih osnovanijah etimologičeskogo analiza", *Voprosy jazykoznanija* (1960), 44-59.

Trubetzkoy, N. S., "Gedanken über das Indogermanenproblem", *Acta Linguistica*, 1 (1939), 81-89.

Uspenskij, B. A., *Strukturnaja tipologija jazykov* (Moskva, 1965).

Voegelin, C. F., Ramanujan, A. K., and Voegelin, F. M., "Typology of Density Ranges", I, "Introduction", *International Journal of American Linguistics*, 26 (1960), 195-197.

Vogt, H., "Language Contacts", *Word*, 10 (1954), 365-374.

Weinreich, U., *Languages in Contact* (New York, 1953).

——, "Is a Structural Dialectology Possible?", *Word*, 10 (1954), 388-400.

——, "On the Description of Phonic Interference", *Word*, 13 (1957), 1 ff.

——, "On the Compatibility of Genetic Relationship and Convergent Development", *Word*, 14 (1958), 374-379.

Wenker, G., *Sprachatlas von Nord und Mitteldeutschland* (Marburg an der Lahn, 1881, etc.).

Wenker, G., and Wrede, F., *Sprachatlas des Deutschen Reichs* (Marburg an der Lahn, 1895, etc.).

Witte, A. J. J., "The Relations of Symbolic and Comparative Linguistics", *Actes du XIᵉ Congrès International de Philosophie*, V, "Logique" (Amsterdam, 1953), 176-179.

Wyatt Jr., W. F., "Structural Linguistics and the Laryngeal Theory", *Language*, 40 (1964), 138-152.

INDEX

AUTHORS REFERRED TO IN THE NOTES